The
Cold War Years

The
Cold War Years

Dale Anderson

RAINTREE
STECK-VAUGHN
RSVP PUBLISHERS

A Harcourt Company

Austin · New York
www.steck-vaughn.com

Published by Raintree Steck-Vaughn Publishers, an imprint of Steck-Vaughn Company

Developed by Discovery Books
Editor: Sabrina Crewe
Designer: Sabine Beaupré
Maps: Stefan Chabluk

Raintree Steck-Vaughn Publishers Staff
Publishing Director: Walter Kossmann
Art Director: Max Brinkmann
Editor: Shirley Shalit

Consultant Andrew Frank, California State University, Los Angeles

Library of Congress Cataloging-in-Publication Data
Anderson, Dale, 1953-
    The Cold War years / Dale Anderson.
        p. cm. -- (The making of America)
    Includes bibliographical references and index.
    ISBN 0-8172-5711-X
    1. United States--History--1945--Juvenile literature. 2. United States--
Social conditions--1945--Juvenile literature. 3. Cold War--Social aspects--
United States--Juvenile literature. 4. United States--Politics and government--
1945-1989--Juvenile literature. [1. United States--History--1945- 2. United
States--Social conditions--1945- 3. Cold War. 4. United States-- Politics and
government--1945-1989.] I. Title. II. Making of America (Austin, Tex.)

E741 .A69 2001
973.92--dc21

                                                                00-062827

Printed and bound in the United States of America
1 2 3 4 5 6 7 8 9 0 IP 04 03 02 01 00

Acknowledgments
Cover AP/Wide World Photos; all other photos Corbis.

Cover illustration: A group of civil rights supporters take part in the March on Washington, a peaceful protest that took place in Washington, D.C., in August 1963.

Contents

Introduction

In 1945, the United States was recovering from two recent crises. The Great Depression that had begun in 1929 had caused tremendous hardship for millions of people. In the course of the Depression, the federal government had grown enormously. The government was not only bigger, but played a more important role in American life than ever before.

It was not until the United States entered World War II in 1941 that the nation really emerged from the Depression. The next four years were a long struggle: Millions of American soldiers went abroad to fight, and millions at home worked to provide weapons and supplies for the war.

World War II was followed by a period of great economic prosperity. Those good times were not shared by all, however. Groups that were denied some part of the American dream began to fight for their rights. This struggle split the country.

The first 30 years after the end of World War II were also a time of great change, often dominated by events in foreign lands. Wartime cooperation with the communist Soviet Union gave way to intense competition. The United States and the Soviet Union, known as the "superpowers," struggled to influence events around the world. Each wanted to enlist other countries to support its political and economic systems. There was no actual warfare between the two superpowers, but the tension was real. The conflict became known as the "Cold War."

The struggle against communism turned to real warfare in Korea and Vietnam. There, American troops fought communist forces, and these wars resulted in thousands of American deaths. Vietnam had a profound effect on Americans at home, where bitter disagreement over the war divided society.

The Cold War Begins

Although the Allied nations together defeated the enemy Axis nations in World War II, their wartime alliance had been one of necessity, not choice. Many issues divided the United States and the Soviet Union, the two main Allied powers. Within just a few years, these two nations were locked in a bitter struggle. Because their armies never fired a single shot at each other, this period of conflict was called the "Cold War." It began in about 1948 and lasted for more than 40 years. In the opening years of this conflict, relations between the two nations were especially poor.

Differing Systems of Government

The Cold War arose from many causes. Basically, though, it was due to the fact that the United States and the Soviet Union had differing views of the world and different goals for the postwar period.

Many in the United States believed in the idea of "One World." In this view, powerful nations would no longer dominate smaller nations. Instead, each nation would be free and independent, and an international organization— the United Nations—would settle disputes between nations and ensure peace. Other countries would also follow the American ideal of a free market, an economy in which businesses can compete with each other without government control. The United States believed its society was superior to others and that other nations would be better off if they followed the American example. In addition, free markets would be good for business. American companies would compete well in world trade because European industries had been badly damaged in World War II.

The Soviet Union, however, was a communist society, meaning it followed a system in which property and resources are owned by the nation as a whole and production is controlled by the national government. This was in direct opposition to the capitalist system in America and other non-communist countries, where businesses and production were mostly privately owned and controlled. The Soviets wanted to impose communism on the countries they dominated. They also wanted security along their borders. If they controlled Poland, Hungary, Czechoslovakia, and Rumania (all countries bordering or close to the Soviet Union), they would have a buffer zone protecting them from other, non-communist nations.

The United Nations

The United Nations (UN) was officially formed on June 26, 1945, when 50 nations signed its charter. Today, about 190 nations belong. All members have a seat in the General Assembly, which is the main body of the United Nations and is responsible for its policies. However, much UN work, such as the settling of international disputes, is carried on in the 15-member Security Council. Five nations—the United States, Russia (which replaced the Soviet Union after the Cold War), Britain, France, and China—are permanent members of the Security Council. Each of these nations has veto power: If any of them votes "no" on a proposal, it will not go into effect. The remaining ten seats on the Security Council are held by other nations on a rotating basis. The UN also has many special agencies. These include the World Health Organization and the United Nations Children's Fund.

The first session of the United Nations General Assembly, taking place in London, England, in 1946.

Agreements and Disagreements

United States President Franklin Roosevelt, the Soviet Union's Joseph Stalin, and Britain's Winston Churchill, known as the "Big Three," met several times during World War II. They reached some agreements about the postwar world at their meetings. In 1944, Roosevelt and Churchill discussed dividing Germany into zones of occupation after World War II. At the Yalta Conference of February 1945, the Big Three agreed to the creation of the United Nations.

The Allies were unable to agree on other issues, however. At Yalta, Stalin wanted Germany to pay billions of dollars in compensation for the damage done to Soviet cities and factories during World War II. Churchill and Roosevelt disagreed. On the issue of new governments in Europe, the leaders reached a vague compromise. They agreed to free elections that would include both pro-American and pro-Soviet candidates. But they made no plans for when and where those elections would occur. Meanwhile, Stalin's troops occupied Poland, and he placed a communist government in power there.

Just two months after Yalta, Franklin Roosevelt died, and Harry Truman became president. Truman believed that Stalin could not be trusted. He began to talk tough, scolding the Soviet foreign minister over the Polish situation. But talking tough was about all he could do. Americans had no desire for more war. The United States did have an advantage, however: It was the only nation with atomic weapons. Truman hoped that the threat of atomic destruction would keep the Soviets from getting too aggressive.

In June 1945, after the war was over in Europe, the division of Germany was established. Britain, the Soviet Union, the United States, and France would each control one part of Germany. Even Berlin, the nation's capital that fell into the Soviet zone, was divided into four sections. In July 1945, Truman met with Stalin and Churchill in Potsdam, Germany. Stalin made some small concessions on Poland, and Truman agreed officially to recognize the

"I believe that it must be the policy of the United States to support free peoples who are resisting attempted subjugation by armed minorities or by outside pressures."

President Harry Truman, speech to Congress, March 12, 1947

pro-Soviet government there. He still refused to let the Soviets claim money for war damages, though. Instead, the Allies agreed to Stalin's demand for billions of dollars worth of equipment and materials from all the zones of Germany to be taken to the Soviet Union.

The Struggle for European Control

Throughout 1946, tensions mounted as the Soviet Union continued to gain control in Eastern Europe. Some of Truman's advisers argued that the Soviets were determined to rule the world. In March 1947, Truman announced a policy called "containment," which aimed to use U.S. power and aid to contain, or limit, Soviet expansion.

Three months later, another new policy was announced. In a June 1947 speech, Secretary of State George Marshall proposed a new program of massive American aid to war-torn Europe. Europe was in miserable condition after the war, and American leaders feared that further hardship would lead to communist takeovers in Western Europe. The European Recovery Program, or Marshall Plan, promised money to any nation in Europe that wanted it. The Soviet Union and its Eastern European allies immediately turned down the offer. Sixteen other nations accepted, however, and within three years the United States had sent more than $13 billion in aid to these nations. Their economies revived, and support for communism in those countries faded.

But tension rose again in 1948. Communists had taken control of the national government of Czechoslovakia, alarming the United States and its allies. Truman decided that the divided zones of Germany made it a weak barrier against Soviet expansion. Britain and France agreed to unite their occupied zones of Germany with the U.S.-controlled zone. These three areas now formed a single republic, which came to be called West Germany. At the same time,

President Harry Truman (center), British Prime Minister Winston Churchill (left), and Soviet leader Joseph Stalin (right) shake hands at the Potsdam Conference in July 1945.

Truman offered aid to Yugoslavia. This nation, although it was communist-controlled, had declared itself independent of Stalin.

Annoyed, Stalin struck back. In June 1948, he blocked transportation routes into the non-Soviet areas of Berlin, known as West Berlin. Because Berlin was deep within Soviet-controlled East Germany, 2 million West Berliners were threatened with starvation. Truman ordered American planes to bring food and supplies to West Berlin by air. For the next ten months, British and American airplanes arrived night and day in an operation called the "Berlin Airlift." In the spring of 1949, Stalin finally ended his blockade.

Children perched on top of rubble in war-torn West Berlin wave to an American cargo plane bringing supplies during the Soviet Union's blockade of 1948 and 1949. At its peak, the Berlin Airlift brought thousands of tons of supplies a day in several hundred landings.

NATO and the Warsaw Pact

In April 1949, the United States formed the North Atlantic Treaty Organization (NATO) with 11 other nations. These were Belgium, Britain, Canada, Denmark, France, Iceland, Italy, Luxembourg, the Netherlands, Norway, and Portugal. The NATO countries agreed that any attack on one member nation would be considered an attack on all, and all would come to that nation's defense. NATO was the first formal alliance the United States had entered into since signing one with France in the 1770s. The NATO nations came to be called, as a group, "the West."

Europe in 1955

miles
0   300
0   km   300

N

UN Members in Europe Outside of NATO and
Warsaw Pact in 1955

NATO Nation Outside of UN in 1955

Members of UN and NATO in 1955

Warsaw Pact Nation Outside of UN in 1955

Members of UN and Warsaw Pact in 1955

Nation Outside of UN, NATO, and Warsaw Pact
in 1955

ICELAND

ATLANTIC
OCEAN

FINLAND

NORWAY

SWEDEN

NORTH
SEA

BRITAIN

DENMARK

IRELAND

SOVIET
UNION

NETHERLANDS

Berlin
EAST
GERMANY

POLAND

BELGIUM

LUXEMBOURG

WEST
GERMANY

CZECHOSLOVAKIA

FRANCE

SWITZERLAND

AUSTRIA

HUNGARY

RUMANIA

PORTUGAL

YUGOSLAVIA

BLACK
SEA

SPAIN

ITALY

BULGARIA

MEDITERRANEAN
SEA

ALBANIA

GREECE

TURKEY

Out of World War II came new international alliances. Ten nations in Europe joined with the United States and Canada to form NATO, while eight communist nations signed the Warsaw Pact.

In May 1955, the Soviet Union joined with the communist nations of Poland, Hungary, Czechoslovakia, Bulgaria, Rumania, Albania, and East Germany in an agreement, negotiated in Warsaw, Poland, called the Warsaw Pact. The Warsaw Pact nations were known as "the East." The world powers had now formed two camps.

Harry S. Truman (1884–1972)

Harry Truman overcame many obstacles to become president. His family suffered from the failure of his father's business ventures, and Truman learned the hard life of farm work. Like his father, he failed as a businessman, but army service in World War I taught Truman that he was a leader and showed him a world beyond his native Missouri.

In the early 1920s, Truman ran for county office. He won easily and served well for eight years. Truman was rewarded in 1934 by winning election to the United States Senate. In the 1944 presidential campaign, Democratic party leaders chose Truman as Franklin Roosevelt's running mate. They won an easy election, but Roosevelt died just five months later. Harry Truman—who called himself "a failure as a farmer and a merchant"—became president.

What kind of president he would be was shown by a sign Truman placed on his desk. "The buck stops here," it said. He was ready for the responsibilities of the presidency. A combative politician and fierce campaigner, Truman always spoke his mind. More than 20 years after his term ended, a biography of Truman was published. It was called, appropriately, *Plain Speaking*.

Communism in China

In the 1940s, communism was also making gains in Asia. The struggle in China had begun in 1927. A communist revolutionary leader named Mao Zedong had rebelled against the nationalist government of Chiang Kai-shek. The two sides fought a bitter civil war, although they set aside their differences to fight a common enemy after Japan invaded China in 1939. Once World War II ended, however, they resumed fighting.

The United States supported Chiang even though his government was corrupt and he was losing the support of the Chinese people. After the war, American money and weapons poured in, but Mao gained ground. In 1949, he won control of the country. Chiang and the nationalists fled to the island of Formosa (now Taiwan). There they set up a new government and called themselves the Republic of China. Mao proclaimed the mainland as the People's Republic of China. In the United States, critics railed at Truman for "losing China" to the communists.

War in Korea

Only eight months later, the United States began to fight again in Asia. The battle zone was Korea, a peninsula that touched northeastern China and lay near Japan. At the end of World War II, the nation had been divided into northern and southern halves. A Soviet-backed communist government ruled in the North and a pro-U.S. dictator ruled in the South. On June 24, 1950, the North Korean army invaded South Korea.

Stronger and better equipped, the North Koreans quickly swept away the South Korean forces. Truman immediately ordered American ships and troops to help South Korea. He asked the United Nations to authorize military action against North Korea. Truman was lucky. The Soviet Union at the time was boycotting the United Nations because the UN— led by the United States—refused to allow Mao's communist government to take China's seat. As a result, there was no Soviet representative to veto the sending of UN troops. The resolution passed, and U.S. General Douglas MacArthur was placed in command of the mostly American UN forces.

An amphibious craft, which could travel on both water and land, arrives at the shore of South Korea in December 1950. This landing of American troops and equipment took place at the beginning of United Nations involvement in the area. The war would continue for two and a half years.

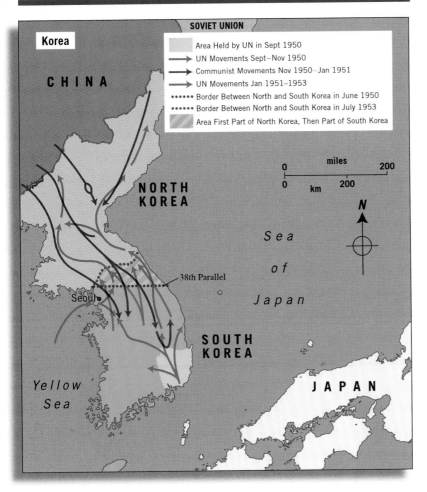

Korea

SOVIET UNION

░░░	Area Held by UN in Sept 1950
→	UN Movements Sept–Nov 1950
→	Communist Movements Nov 1950–Jan 1951
→	UN Movements Jan 1951–1953
••••	Border Between North and South Korea in June 1950
▪▪▪▪	Border Between North and South Korea in July 1953
▨	Area First Part of North Korea, Then Part of South Korea

CHINA

NORTH KOREA

Sea of Japan

38th Parallel

Seoul

SOUTH KOREA

Yellow Sea

JAPAN

miles 0 — 200
km 0 — 200

N

United Nations forces, starting from their toehold on the southeastern tip of Korea, pushed up into the communist North in 1950. But by early 1951, they had been driven back by communist troops. By the time a truce was signed in 1953, the communists had retreated again and a border between North and South was established north of the original boundary.

When MacArthur arrived on the scene, UN troops held only a small area in southeastern Korea. MacArthur ordered a surprise attack near the border with North Korea. He hoped to get behind the North Korean lines and force them to pull back. The plan was a brilliant success. UN troops drove their enemy back into North Korea. In October 1950, Truman again won UN backing, this time for an invasion of the North aimed at creating "a unified, independent, and democratic Korea." At first, the UN forces enjoyed continued success. Then, soldiers from communist China entered the war, and American troops found themselves fighting Chinese troops. The UN forces were pushed back south again. The two sides then settled into a long stalemate.

American leaders disagreed on what to do next. MacArthur wanted to bomb Chinese troops in China. Truman turned down his plan, fearing that a direct attack on China would start a world war. MacArthur then took his idea to the public, who at first supported him rather than the president. In April 1951, MacArthur was fired for disobeying the president, who is commander in chief of the armed forces. Critics said Truman was not being tough enough, but public opinion shifted back to support him rather than the general.

McCarthy and the Red Scare

Communism now had a strong foothold in Europe and Asia. Meanwhile, many Americans were determined to remove what they saw as the threat of communism at home. In a period known as the "Red Scare," a growing hysteria led

Espionage

The House Un-American Activities Committee (HUAC) was originally set up in 1938 to investigate extreme political organizations operating in America. In 1948, during the Red Scare, a case of espionage, or spying for an enemy, was brought before HUAC. Whittaker Chambers, an editor for *Time* magazine, told HUAC that he had been a member of the Communist party in the 1930s. At that time, he said, State Department employee Alger Hiss had also been a communist. Chambers charged that Hiss had given him secret government papers. Hiss denied the charges, but Chambers produced filmed copies of the papers. Hiss was tried and convicted in 1950 of lying to Congress.

Even worse, Americans learned that secrets about nuclear weapons were being given away. In 1949, President Truman announced to the American people that the Soviet Union had successfully tested an atomic bomb. The next year, a British scientist named Klaus Fuchs said that he had given the Soviets information some years before that allowed them to develop their bomb. Two members of the American Communist party, Julius and Ethel Rosenberg, were suspected of helping. The Rosenbergs were found guilty of espionage in 1951 and sentenced to death. They were executed in 1953.

people to view their fellow citizens with suspicion. Several events led some people to believe that the Democrats had let communists into the American government. Truman had tried to combat this idea. In 1947, he established a program to investigate the loyalty of workers in the federal government.

In the midst of rising fears of communism, a new voice arose. Joseph McCarthy was a first-term senator from Wisconsin who had done little to distinguish himself. In a speech in Wheeling, West Virginia, in February 1950, McCarthy announced that he had a list of 205 known communists who worked in the State Department. In truth, he had no list, nor did he know for certain that there were 205 communists in the State Department.

The fact that he was lying did not stop McCarthy from becoming a very powerful figure. His charges created a sensation. Reporters printed stories showing that McCarthy had no evidence for this charge nor for others he made later in the Senate. Yet polls showed that a majority of Americans believed him, and other politicians had to reckon with his growing power. For the next two years, McCarthy dominated American politics.

McCarthy's tactics came to be called "McCarthyism." He loudly charged people with being communists even when he had no proof. When challenged, he often lessened the charge from communism to a vague term like "disloyalty." Whatever the charge, people's reputations suffered. Many were forced to quit their jobs, and lives were ruined. Few politicians stood up to McCarthy. Even the hugely popular Dwight Eisenhower, a candidate for the presidency in 1952, said nothing when McCarthy accused George Marshall, Eisenhower's friend and commander during World War II, of disloyalty.

During the Red Scare, many show business professionals were called to testify about their beliefs and those of colleagues before the House Un-American Activities Committee (HUAC). In this photo, movie stars Lauren Bacall and Humphrey Bogart lead a protest against the HUAC hearings in the late 1940s.

"I have here in my hand a list of 205 [people] that were known to the Secretary of State as being members of the Communist party and are still working and shaping the policy of the State Department."

Senator Joseph McCarthy, 1950

17

In 1954, after Eisenhower had become president, McCarthy's power was finally broken. The senator had charged that communists were in the armed forces, and the Senate allowed him to investigate. The Army-McCarthy Hearings, as they were called, were televised, and they revealed McCarthy as little more than a bully. People saw him harass witnesses and give evasive answers to questions put to him. Approval of McCarthy plunged, and in December 1954, the Senate voted to censure him for "conduct unbecoming a senator."

A New Leader

The Republican Eisenhower was opposed in 1952 by the Democrat Adlai Stevenson, governor of Illinois. Stevenson was no match for Eisenhower, however, who promised to "go to Korea" to end the war. Eisenhower won the presidency in a landslide, and Republicans took control of both houses of Congress.

In June 1953, after Eisenhower took office, talks in Korea finally produced a cease-fire agreement. The agreement stopped the fighting but fell short of a true end to the conflict. Tens of thousands of American troops remained stationed in Korea to help maintain the weak truce.

Eisenhower continued Truman's policy of containment. His secretary of state, John Foster Dulles, also announced a new policy, called "massive retaliation." Any threats to America's allies, he said, would be met with massive— meaning nuclear—force. Early in 1954, President Eisenhower revealed that the United States had tested a nuclear weapon even more powerful than the atomic bombs that had been used in Japan in 1945. (The dropping of the bombs by the Allies had brought an end to World War II.) These new hydrogen bombs could destroy an area of 700 square miles (1,800 sq km). But the American monopoly on this new weapon didn't last out the year. The Soviet Union announced its own hydrogen bomb, and the two superpowers began a long and expensive arms race.

Aggression Abroad

While they talked of massive retaliation, Eisenhower and Dulles struck first on a small scale. Iran is an oil-rich nation in the Middle East, and in 1953 Eisenhower feared that country was beginning to favor the Soviet Union over the West. The United States intervened in Iran that year, when the Central Intelligence Agency (CIA) helped a group of army officers overthrow the government. The next year, the CIA unseated a new government with Soviet sympathies in Guatemala.

These events took place against a backdrop of better relations with the Soviet Union. In 1953, Joseph Stalin had died. In 1955, Eisenhower and NATO leaders met with the new Soviet leader, Nikita Khrushchev, in Geneva, Switzerland, and felt there was a willingness to cooperate.

The promising "spirit of Geneva" did not last long, however. At a follow-up meeting, the West and East could reach no agreements. Then, in 1956, Hungarians rose up and demanded democratic reforms. They overthrew the communists and gained control of their own government. But Soviet tanks rolled into the country and restored the communists to power. Eisenhower dashed the rebels' hopes when he sent no aid.

Sputnik

Until 1957, Americans viewed the Soviets as technologically backward. The Soviet Union did have nuclear weapons, but the United States believed that they achieved this by stealing secrets. American scientists, they were sure, were superior to Soviet ones.

In 1957, however, the Soviets announced that they had launched a satellite called *Sputnik*. The launch required the use of massive rocket power, enough to send nuclear weapons to the United

President Eisenhower stands in front of a microphone as Nikita Khrushchev (right of Eisenhower) raises his hat to spectators. The Soviet leader was starting a 12-day tour of the United States in 1959. Khrushchev was an energetic man who tried to make some reforms in the Soviet government, and it seemed he was also more ready to establish good relations with the West. However, beneath the friendly surface, opposing ideals kept the Cold War simmering.

States. The Portland *Oregonian* said, "It is downright terrifying with [*Sputnik*] staring down at us." The Soviet triumph looked even better the next year, when the United States tried to launch its own first satellite, and the rocket exploded.

President Eisenhower calmly faced a storm of criticism about *Sputnik*. He knew that the Soviets were, in fact, behind the United States in the development of missiles. He knew this because American U-2 spy planes had been flying over the Soviet Union taking pictures of military facilities. But those flights were illegal because they violated Soviet air space, and he could not reveal them.

That secret came out in 1960, when the Soviet Union shot down an American U-2 plane over its territory. At first, the American government denied that the plane had been on a spy mission. When the Soviets produced the pilot, however, Eisenhower was forced to admit the truth. Khrushchev angrily cancelled a planned meeting with Eisenhower. The Cold War was raging more fiercely than ever.

50 Years of NATO

In 1999, NATO celebrated its 50th anniversary. NATO appeared to be a tremendous success. It had achieved its main goal, that of defending the West against communism. In fact, by 1999, communism had collapsed in Europe. The Soviet Union had broken apart. NATO had grown to include 19 nations. Three of them—the Czech Republic, Poland, and Hungary—had once been part of the Warsaw Pact.

However, just one month earlier, NATO had gone to war. The Serbian leader of Yugoslavia had carried out a series of attacks against Albanians in Kosovo, a part of Yugoslavia. Outraged by these attacks, and after failed negotiations, NATO began to bomb Yugoslavia. President Bill Clinton said that NATO fought "because the alliance will not have meaning in the twenty-first century if it permits the slaughter of innocents on its doorstep." Despite its power, NATO did not win a quick victory, and Albanian suffering worsened considerably. Eventually, due to continued NATO bombing, the Serbs pulled out and allowed the Albanians to return home.

Prosperity and Change

Although the United States was engaged in the tense Cold War, it experienced an amazing period of economic growth. A generation that had grown up in the Great Depression and World War II suddenly found prosperity. This period brought huge changes to American society.

A Peacetime Economy

Government officials thought that the change from a wartime to a peacetime economy was going to be difficult. They feared that the nation could be plunged into another depression. They were wrong about that, but they were right that the road would not be smooth. One reason was that World War II in the Pacific ended sooner than expected, in August 1945 (only three months after the war's end in Europe). As a result, there had been little government planning for the new economy. Another cause was the American people themselves. After years of upheaval, they wanted life to go back to normal as quickly as possible.

Many feared that the shift in industry to peacetime production would cause an economic slowdown. However, consumer spending shot up. During the war, people had been earning high wages but had little to

During World War II, automobile factories were converted for the production of tanks, weapons, and other military equipment. When the war ended, manufacturers quickly returned to making cars, such as this Dodge from a 1947 advertisement, that were in high demand by consumers.

21

buy because production was devoted to military goods. With the war over, they started buying.

Another factor that spurred spending was the GI Bill. Officially called the Servicemen's Readjustment Act of 1944, the law aimed to help returning soldiers resume civilian life. It provided unemployment payments, low-cost housing loans, and aid for college or vocational education to veterans of the war. Millions of former soldiers used GI Bill money to go to college and buy a house.

Truman's Policies

All this consumer spending caused inflation, however. Prices shot up by as much as 15 percent a year. President Truman was forced to put price controls in place. Truman also hoped to push a series of reforms through Congress. He wanted to raise the minimum wage, improve housing, give federal dollars for education, and establish a nationwide system of health insurance. Truman presented his program in 1945, calling it the "Fair Deal." It continued the work of the New Deal introduced in 1933 by President Roosevelt.

The prospects for this program were poor. Republicans in control of Congress didn't pass any of Truman's pet projects. Instead, they passed the Taft-Hartley Act in 1947, which aimed to weaken the power of labor unions. Truman vetoed the bill, but Congress overrode his veto.

Truman ran for reelection in 1948, when few people thought he had a chance of winning. He campaigned hard, however, traveling 32,000 miles (51,500 km) and making more than 350 speeches. In each, he blasted the "do-nothing, good-for-nothing" Republicans in Congress. To the nation's surprise, Truman won. Truman was still unable to convince Congress to pass the laws he wanted, but he did make some progress in an area important to him: civil rights.

Stirrings for Civil Rights

When Truman became president, segregation existed in the United States. This meant that African American citizens, in particular those living in Southern states, were deliberately kept separate from whites and were denied certain basic rights. Segregation was achieved by various means. African Americans served in all-black units in the military. Black students were denied education in some white schools and colleges. Public places, such as restaurants and theaters, either refused access to blacks or had separate entrances and facilities. In certain states, laws supported segregation; in others, it was the general attitude of whites to blacks that created inequality between the races.

In 1948, Truman called for an end to segregation in the armed forces. Truman also ordered an end to racial discrimination by the federal government. He wanted to go further and make a federal crime of lynching, the killing of black people by white mobs that took place mostly in the South. At the time, state officials never acted to punish lynch mobs. Truman also hoped to support African American efforts to overcome Southern laws that made it difficult for them to vote (see page 41). But Congress would not pass his bills.

These moves produced a political backlash. In 1948, Southern Democrats broke from the party to protest Truman's steps toward racial equality. They formed their own party, the Dixiecrats. ("Dixie" was a traditional name for the South.) They ran their own candidate, J. Strom Thurmond, for president in 1948. It was the beginning of a long process during which the Democrats lost the support of many Southern whites.

African Americans slowly chipped away at the segregation laws that denied them equality. The National Association for the Advancement of Colored People (NAACP) had a special unit of lawyers to challenge laws blocking rights for blacks. They won several cases. In 1946, the Supreme Court ruled that an African American could not be required to give up his or

Although this black student was allowed to attend a college class with whites, he was required to sit outside the classroom. This kind of discrimination, widely accepted in the South, spurred the first civil rights activists of the late 1940s and early 1950s.

her seat to a white passenger on a bus that traveled between states. A ruling in Oklahoma forced a state university to admit an African American woman as a student.

African Americans also made gains in this period from the fame won by certain talented individuals. Diplomat Ralph Bunche, at the United Nations, helped negotiate a limited peace in the long-running conflict between Israel and its Arab neighbors. For his efforts, Bunche won a Nobel Peace Prize.

Of greater symbolic importance was an advance in sports. Although African Americans had played professional baseball in the sport's early years, owners of major league teams began to ban black players in the late 1800s. For more than half a century, African Americans had been kept out of major league baseball. That changed in 1947, when Jackie Robinson began to play for a major league team. Soon, other teams signed black players. The integration of the nation's favorite sport broke a psychological barrier for Americans.

The Eisenhower Years

In 1952, Republican Dwight D. Eisenhower was swept into the presidency by a strong majority. Nicknamed "Ike," he was a comfortable, grandfatherly figure who contrasted with Truman. Most of all, Eisenhower was a moderate. He didn't want Truman's aggressive Fair Deal reforms, but he was unwilling to support those who hoped to undo the earlier New Deal policies. And although he was concerned that the push for civil rights could divide the country, he acted to uphold federal court decisions in favor of equal rights. He worked for the politics of consensus, which means following policies backed by most Americans.

Eisenhower filled his Cabinet, which is made up of the leaders of government departments, with people in business. Charles Wilson, who became secretary of defense, was the president of General Motors. Another Cabinet member had been head of a financial firm. The Cabinet firmly supported policies that were favorable to American business and economic growth.

"For years I thought what was good for our country was good for General Motors and vice versa."

Charles Wilson,
January 1953

Jackie Robinson (1919–72)

Teammates and opponents admired Jackie Robinson's talent and his fierce will to win in baseball. But Jackie Robinson was also a revolutionary. He changed the face of American sports and in this way helped change American society.

At the University of California, Robinson was a star athlete who excelled at many sports. In the army, he challenged the prejudice faced by African Americans. He refused to play on a base football team because some opposing teams would not play against blacks.

Branch Rickey, president of the National League baseball team the Brooklyn Dodgers, decided he would break the ban that kept black players out of the major leagues. He chose Robinson to be the first black player because of his skills, his college education, and his self-control. Rickey warned the player that he would face insults and harassment. Robinson agreed not to fight back for a year. He would not give racists a chance to find any fault with him.

Robinson's first year with the Dodgers, 1947, was a struggle. He endured pitches thrown at his head, rough tags from opposing fielders, and insults from opponents and fans. Robinson responded by helping his team to the National League championship and winning the Rookie of the Year award. Over the years, he helped the Dodgers win six pennants and one World Series. Robinson retired in 1956. He was elected to the Hall of Fame in 1962, the first year he was eligible.

"We conclude that in the field of public education the doctrine of 'separate but equal' has no place. Separate educational facilities are . . . unequal."

U.S. Supreme Court, Brown v. Board of Education of Topeka *ruling, 1954*

Most Americans didn't object to this pro-business approach. For many, the 1950s was a time of prosperity and economic success. Per-capita income—the average that each worker earns—rose by almost 40 percent from 1945 to 1960. Family income rose even more. For many, but not all, the 1950s were an economic bonanza.

Civil Rights Grow

Civil rights gained new ground during Eisenhower's presidency. The NAACP's biggest court victory came in 1954, when the U.S. Supreme Court issued its ruling *Brown v. Board of Education of Topeka.* The NAACP lawyers argued that the rights of an African American girl from Kansas were denied because the all-black school she was sent to was not as good as the school white students attended. The Court ruled unanimously in the student's favor. All nine justices said that schools had to be integrated.

Eisenhower was uncomfortable with the *Brown* decision as he felt that integration in Southern schools would be difficult. But he ordered the integration of all schools in the District of Columbia, an area controlled by the federal government. Many school systems worked quietly to put the decision into practice, but many more dragged their feet, and opposition to integration grew. Some Southern members of Congress banded together to urge people in the South to disobey the *Brown* decision.

In September 1957, nine black students were to start attending high school in Little Rock, Arkansas. When the state's governor, Orval Faubus, defied a federal court order that the children be admitted, President Eisenhower sent in federal troops so that the students could enter the school.

Thurgood Marshall (1908–93)

Heading the team of NAACP lawyers who argued *Brown v. Board of Education of Topeka* was Thurgood Marshall. Born in Baltimore, Maryland, Marshall grew up going to segregated schools. He later recalled that he was frequently punished in elementary school. His punishment was to read the Constitution. "Before I left school, I knew the Constitution by heart," he said. That knowledge later served him well.

Thurgood Marshall in front of the U.S. Supreme Court building with fellow attorneys George Hayes (left) and James Nabrit (right) after their victory in the Brown *decision.*

Marshall graduated first in his class at Howard University Law School in 1933. A few years later, he joined the NAACP's legal staff. In 1940, he became head of the group's team of lawyers. Marshall devised the strategy of challenging segregation laws, especially in education. He brought cases before the Supreme Court 32 times and won 29 of them.

Marshall served as the United States Solicitor General from 1965 to 1967. He was then appointed to the Supreme Court, becoming the first African American justice. Marshall served until his retirement in 1991.

Suburban Life

One of the biggest changes that affected America after World War II was a population shift from cities to suburbs. Along with that shift came major changes in American society.

Also, with the return of servicemen from the war, Americans began having more children, a trend called the "baby boom." The population shot up by nearly 20 percent from 1950 to 1960. But there was a housing shortage because new building had been stalled for years by the Depression and the war. A giant construction boom began. Across the country, contractors began building thousands of houses that growing families flocked to buy. Because of the GI Bill, buying houses became easier for World War II veterans.

Suddenly, suburbs were springing up across the United States. The suburbs were cleaner and neater than the cities. Each house had a yard, and the curving streets made for a pleasant appearance. Builders put in small parks and playgrounds, and towns added new schools. The suburbs were a great place to raise those growing American families.

There was another reason for the rush to the suburbs. More and more African Americans were moving to cities, especially in the North. With the Supreme Court's *Brown* decision, the push was on to integrate schools, and many whites moved to the suburbs to avoid this.

Levittowns

William Levitt spurred the housing boom by inventing mass-produced housing. Levitt had used mass production to build military housing, airfields, and buildings during World War II. In that time, he perfected the technique of breaking construction into steps and using rotating teams to complete those steps as quickly as possible.

After the war, Levitt applied the idea to homes for civilians. First, a work crew laid all the foundations. Another crew put up the frameworks, different teams did electrical and plumbing work, and yet others finished the walls and interiors. Levitt's houses, though small, seemed like a dream—an inexpensive dream. They sold for less than $10,000. The first day his houses went on sale, Levitt signed contracts with 1,400 buyers.

Cities didn't have enough land for Levitt's houses, so he located them on the outskirts, forming new suburbs. The first Levittown was on Long Island, New York. Soon, other builders took up his techniques, and similar suburbs followed.

The first Levittown on Long Island, New York.

Consumer Culture

By 1960, one-third of all Americans lived in suburbs. And they were generating a new American culture based on the mobility provided by cars. The suburbs had no mass transit systems, as cities did, and houses were more spread out. To get around, people had to drive. Car sales shot up, and merchants found new ways of attracting suburban drivers.

While the auto industry churned out more and more cars, other industries produced washing machines, dishwashers, and other domestic appliances. These labor-saving devices made it easier to run a home and persuaded Americans to continue their consumer spending.

The Birth of Television

In 1946, there were only 17,000 television sets in the entire country. By 1953, there were sets in two-thirds of all American homes. Hugely popular shows, with stars such as Milton Berle and Lucille Ball, drew audiences of up to 50 million viewers by 1954. Television helped promote the consumer culture that was growing throughout the 1950s. Shows were sponsored by the companies that made cars, cigarettes, appliances, soaps, and many other products. Advertising on TV urged Americans to spend, spend, spend.

The success of television affected other industries. From the 1920s to the 1940s, radio had been the main means of home entertainment, full of comedy, dramas, and variety

The term "drive-in" entered the national vocabulary as restaurants, banks, movie theaters, and other businesses tried to make it easy and quick for customers to use services in their vehicles. This drive-in restaurant in Liberal, Kansas, was one of many that sprang up in the 1950s.

The Lone Ranger (Clayton Moore), seen here with his sidekick Tonto (Jay Silverheels), had been the star of a popular radio show. In the 1950s, "The Lone Ranger" series transferred to television, where it became a long-running hit.

shows. When television took over that role, radio moved to carrying mostly music. And as people stayed at home to watch the small screen, movie ticket sales dropped. Television gave greater popularity to professional and college sports while draining stadiums of ticket buyers who could now watch games at home.

Conformists and Nonconformists

Into the first half of the twentieth century, America had been a land of states and regions. People in one area had distinct foods, customs, and ways of speech. The postwar period helped make those local differences fade. Television, the suburbs, and consumer culture reflected that trend. Millions of people in all areas of the country watched the same television shows, lived in houses that looked the same, and bought the same products. American culture in the 1950s was marked by conformity, meaning that most people wanted to be like other people.

Criticism of this mainstream culture took many forms. Sociologists examined the effects of conformity on the people who were trapped by it. In *White Collar* (1951), sociologist C. Wright Mills charged that Americans were losing their individualism. David Riesman, in *The Lonely Crowd* (1950), said that Americans were abandoning their personal values for group values in order to be accepted. William H. Whyte, in *The Organization Man* (1956), analyzed how large, bureaucratic companies took away the individuality of the people who worked for them.

A group of young artists and writers criticized mainstream culture more loudly. Calling themselves the "Beats," they condemned the culture's sameness and empty consumerism.

Teenagers became a rising force in American society, partly because they were such avid consumers. They spent millions of dollars each year buying clothes, makeup, and records, and going to movies.

Although teenagers were a new generation of consumers, they rebelled against their society in another way. The records they bought in large numbers featured a new sound: rock and roll. Rock grew out of the blues music sung and played by African Americans for decades. The new music, which shocked older generations, exploded across the country in 1955 when a Mississippi-born singer named Elvis Presley hit the scene. The film industry also found ways to make money from teen rebellion, with such movies as *The Wild One* and *Rebel Without a Cause*.

The Struggle for Equality

For millions of people, the United States was a land of plenty and of opportunity. But millions more were haunted by poverty and discrimination. Farm prices dropped, and more and more farmers left their farms for the cities. Many of these former farmers were African American, and their arrival increased the size and number of black communities in urban slums.

Like blacks, Hispanics also suffered discrimination. Thousands of Mexican Americans worked as migrant laborers harvesting the farm crops of the Southwest and California. They lived in appalling conditions and were forced to accept very low wages. Some Hispanics became politically active, including those who organized efforts to register voters in their communities, thereby giving Mexican Americans a voice in the government of their country. The Hispanic community in California won a victory when the state government banned the practice of putting Mexican American children in separate classrooms.

Elvis Presley performed songs that combined black blues with white country music. He moved in a way that parents disliked but their kids loved. Presley's records sold in the millions, and Hollywood signed him up for several movies.

31

Native Americans also became more active. They had formed the National Congress of American Indians in 1944 to campaign for greater control of their own lives. Eventually, the group represented the tribes of about two-thirds of all Native Americans in the country. However, Native Americans were jolted by a change in federal policy in 1953, when the government announced that it would end financial aid to Indian reservations. Thousands of Native Americans were moved to cities in the hope they would adapt to white culture. The policy—a complete failure—was abandoned in 1963.

The Montgomery Bus Boycott

The minority group that made the most advances in the 1950s was African Americans. On December 1, 1955, an African American woman named Rosa Parks was sitting on a bus in Montgomery, Alabama, returning home after a long day's work. The bus was full, and when a white rider entered it, the driver asked Parks to give up her seat. She refused, breaking a city law, and was placed under arrest.

Rosa Parks sits on a bus in Montgomery, Alabama, on December 21, 1956, the day that the Montgomery bus boycott ended. More than a year earlier, Parks's refusal to surrender her seat to a white passenger sparked the boycott.

African American leaders then called a boycott of the city bus system. This was a significant move because blacks accounted for 75 percent of the bus system's riders. The boycott, planned to last just one day, continued day after day. African Americans walked to schools and jobs. They gave each other rides. Some white women drove boycotting black maids to their homes so they could continue to cook and clean. The city government struck back, arresting black leaders and harassing the boycotters.

Early on in the protest, African Americans had chosen as their leader Martin Luther King, Jr., a young minister. His eloquence and determination kept the boycott going, even after he was arrested. The black community held firm for more than a year. Finally, the U.S. Supreme Court ruled in late 1956 that discrimination in public transportation was unconstitutional. With that victory, the boycott ended. After the boycott, King began to dedicate his time fully to the struggle for civil rights. King's leadership was a driving force behind major advances that occurred in the 1960s.

"There comes a time when people get tired of being trampled over by the iron feet of oppression. . . . I want it to be known —that we're going to work with grim and bold determination— to gain justice on buses in this city. And we are not wrong. . . . If we are wrong—the Supreme Court of this nation is wrong. If we are wrong—God Almighty is wrong. . . . If we are wrong— justice is a lie."

Martin Luther King, Jr., Montgomery, Alabama, December 5, 1955

The Disney Empire

Walt Disney and his brother had started a company making cartoons back in 1923. They made several successful movies, and introduced the lovable Mickey Mouse and the cranky Donald Duck.

In the 1950s, Disney expanded into television. Each afternoon, millions of American children gathered in front of their televisions to sing along with the "The Mickey Mouse Club." Along with producing more television shows, the Disney company opened Disneyland in southern California in 1955, drawing large crowds.

In 1971, the company opened a park in Orlando, Florida, called DisneyWorld. The Disney empire went through difficult times in the 1970s and early 1980s as its movies failed, but in the mid-1980s, the company became more successful than ever. It expanded DisneyWorld and opened another park in France. Disney also bought a hockey team and opened more than 500 stores to sell Disney-related products. There was a new round of hit movies, and in 1996, Disney added a TV network and cable stations to its huge media empire.

The New Frontier and the Great Society

I n the last years of the Eisenhower presidency, many
Americans began to feel that the nation was drifting and
in need of firmer government. At the same time, world
events suggested to some that the United States was losing
the Cold War.

Trouble Looms

Sputnik had shaken the United States' confidence in its own
technology. Critics began to speak of a "missile gap," arguing
that the Soviet Union had built more missiles to deliver
nuclear weapons than had the United States. There was
growing news of anti-American demonstrations around the
world. In 1958, Vice President Richard Nixon's car was pelted
with rocks by angry demonstrators in Caracas, Venezuela.

The following year, a new menace appeared closer to
home. In 1959, a rebel named Fidel Castro succeeded in
overthrowing the dictator Fulgencio Batista who ruled Cuba,
an island in the Caribbean just 90 miles (145 km) from the
coast of Florida. At first, the American government did not
object to Castro because his predecessor had been corrupt.
Soon, though, Castro began to seize foreign-owned property in
Cuba, including that owned by American businesses. Relations
with Cuba quickly cooled. In 1960, Castro accepted aid from
the Soviet Union and declared himself a communist. The
Cold War, it seemed, had reached America's backyard.

The 1960 Election

Americans, troubled by these events, were facing a choice in their leadership. 1960 was an election year, and the two presidential candidates were both young and energetic. Both were part of the generation that had fought and won World War II. The Republican candidate was current Vice President Richard Nixon. He offered a long record of tough anti-communism, eight years of experience as vice president, and moderate views on domestic issues.

Opposing Nixon was John F. Kennedy, a second-term Democratic senator from Massachusetts. Kennedy said that it was time for a president who would "get the country moving again." The election was the second closest in history. Kennedy won, but little more than 100,000 votes separated him from Nixon.

The New Frontier

President Kennedy began his presidency with a spirit of national service. He launched an organization called the Peace Corps. The group recruited young, talented American citizens to work as teachers, advisers, and medical staff in undeveloped countries. Soon, thousands of Americans were in Africa, Asia, and Latin America. Kennedy announced another new program called the Alliance for Progress. This plan intended to send aid to the nations of Latin America to prevent them from adopting communism, as Cuba had done.

Kennedy brought to Washington brilliant people with impressive backgrounds. They were confident in their ability to change and improve the world and eager to get started. The new president proclaimed that the United States was about to cross a "New Frontier."

Kennedy hoped to persuade Congress to pass a series of new domestic programs related to housing, medical care,

Central to the 1960 presidential campaign were television debates—the first presidential debates ever televised—between the two candidates. Richard Nixon was seen as the more experienced of the two, but his performance was marred by the fact that he was just recovering from illness. John F. Kennedy looked more vigorous and spoke calmly and forcefully about world and domestic issues.

"Ask not what your country can do for you—ask what you can do for your country."

President John F. Kennedy, inaugural address, January 20, 1960

The Space Race

In spite of battles with Congress over several of his programs, President Kennedy succeeded with one major initiative: the space program. In 1961, Americans were embarrassed when the Soviet Union twice put men into orbit around the Earth. Two Americans, Alan B. Shepard and Virgil Grissom, did make manned space flights in 1961, but they did not orbit the Earth.

President Kennedy followed Shepard's flight with a speech to Congress. He announced a program to put an astronaut on the moon before the end of the decade. Congress approved the plan, but at first the space program continued to trail the Soviet Union's. The first American orbit, by John Glenn, came in February 1962, several months after the Russian missions. The Soviets were also the first to have a man walk in space, in early 1965. The first American, Edward White, did so on June 3, 1965.

A photograph taken by astronaut Neil Armstrong of his colleague Buzz Aldrin on the moon's surface.

Eventually, though, the American space program moved ahead. In late 1968, the first three-man crew reached the moon, which they orbited ten times. On July 20, 1969, humankind reached a milestone. That day, Neil Armstrong and Buzz Aldrin landed their spacecraft on the moon. Millions around the world watched as they beamed back to Earth live pictures of the first human footsteps on the moon.

school funding, and urban affairs. But his narrow margin of victory in the election hampered his ability to do so. The split within his own party didn't help either. Southern Democrats were more conservative than the president, and more likely to join with Republicans. Committees in Congress soon blocked Kennedy's proposals for reform.

Cold War Tensions Renew

The main focus of Kennedy's presidency was foreign affairs. His first foreign policy move was a complete disaster, however. When Kennedy came to office, he found that the American Central Intelligence Agency (CIA) had secretly developed a plan to oust Castro. It had armed and trained a group of Cubans living in the United States. They would land 1,500 men on a Cuban beach and, with support from U.S. planes, launch a rebellion to take over the island. Kennedy approved the plan but then cut off the air support, afraid that the U.S. involvement would be too visible. The invasion of the Bay of Pigs, on the south coast of Cuba, took place on April 17, 1961. As a result of the lack of air support, some of the CIA-trained Cubans were killed and the rest captured. Kennedy realized that he should never have accepted the plan.

This photograph shows how the Berlin Wall sliced right through the German capital, dividing the communist and non-communist nations. On a visit to Berlin in June 1963, President Kennedy (center, by the rail) stood on a platform by the wall to make a speech.

Kennedy worried that the Soviet Union would view the failure at the Bay of Pigs as weakness on his part. He was right. Shortly after, he had a meeting with Khrushchev in which the Soviet leader threatened war.

Then came a new crisis in Berlin. By 1961, thousands of East Germans were leaving their country for West Germany. Many did so by crossing from Soviet-held East Berlin to West Berlin. On August 13, 1961, before dawn, Soviet and East German soldiers began putting up barricades at the border that divided the city.

Within days, the boundary was sealed and patrolled by East German troops. Anyone who tried to cross the Berlin Wall, as it was called, was shot on the spot. Kennedy could do little but protest. He did not want a war over Berlin.

The Cuban Missile Crisis

In 1962, the threat of war seemed much more real. The trouble spot, once again, was Cuba. Photographs from American spy planes revealed that the Soviets were building missile bases there. From these bases, they could launch a nuclear strike against the United States.

Kennedy and his advisers saw the Soviet move as a direct threat. The president announced his policy on October 22, 1962. He put the nation's defenses on alert and reinforced the U.S. naval base at Guantanamo (see map below). Kennedy said that naval and air patrols would prevent any Soviet ship that carried weapons from reaching the island. Finally, he told Khrushchev that the missiles had to be removed from Cuba.

For several days, the world waited to see if the two superpowers would destroy each other in a terrible nuclear battle. Four days after Kennedy's announcement, Khrushchev agreed to remove the missiles as long as the United States promised not to invade Cuba. Kennedy agreed, and the crisis was over. The world breathed easier again.

"We're eyeball to eyeball and I think the other fellow just blinked."

Secretary of State Dean Rusk, after hearing that Soviet ships had withdrawn during the Cuban Missile Crisis, October 24, 1962

Cuba, a former protectorate of the United States, is an island in the Caribbean just 90 miles (145 km) from the Florida coast. During the Cuban Missile Crisis of 1962, Americans felt threatened by the fact that Soviet weapons were so near to the American mainland.

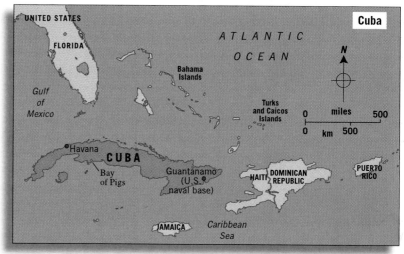

John Kennedy (1917–63)

John F. Kennedy was one of nine children born to a wealthy investor and his wife, the daughter of a prominent Boston politician. He joined the navy in World War II, winning medals for heroism in the Pacific. When he returned to civilian life, Kennedy entered politics. He served three terms in the House of Representatives and was elected to the Senate in 1952. The next year, he married Jacqueline Bouvier, a glamorous socialite.

Kennedy was not a powerful member of Congress. He was an appealing presidential candidate, however, and decided to run for office in 1960. He had three drawbacks: his youth, his inexperience, and the fact that he was a Roman Catholic. No Catholic had ever won the presidency, and the United States had a history of anti-Catholic feeling.

Kennedy won the election in spite of these factors. As president, he enjoyed favorable press coverage, with reporters often noting his charm, wit, and youthful family. His assassination will always be remembered by the people who lived through it. The first years of Kennedy's administration had been a time of optimism and hope. Within a few years of his death, turmoil and violence seemed to plague the country.

After the Cuban Missile Crisis, tensions between the United States and the Soviet Union eased. Kennedy made a speech suggesting that the two nations should avoid conflict and "make the world safe for diversity," meaning for different beliefs and ways of governing. The two countries agreed in August 1963 to a treaty that banned both of them from the testing of nuclear weapons in the atmosphere, in outer space, and under water.

The events in Cuba also had some negative effects. Khrushchev had been forced to back down. Within two years, other Soviet leaders removed him from office and put in place those who took a harder line against the West. Also, the Soviets felt that the missile crisis revealed that they were weaker than the United States. To improve its position, the Soviet Union increased spending on nuclear weapons. The result was a renewed arms race.

Martin Luther King, Jr. (1929–68)

Martin Luther King's father was a Baptist minister, as was his mother's father. After his studies, which gained him a Ph.D. from Boston University in 1955, King entered the ministry himself, as pastor of a Baptist church in Montgomery, Alabama.

The famous Montgomery bus boycott of 1955 and 1956 propelled King into the national spotlight. As one of the founders of the Southern Christian Leadership Conference (SCLC), King created a network of ministers across the South. He taught them the principles of nonviolent civil disobedience. From 1960 to 1965, King and the SCLC led several protests against segregation in the South.

Martin Luther King in jail after one of his many arrests for taking part in civil rights protests.

Sometimes brutally attacked by whites, the SCLC maintained its nonviolent principles. This strongly moral stand and King's moving and eloquent speeches helped stir sympathy for African Americans across the United States and around the world. King made his most famous speech at the March on Washington, a peaceful civil rights protest in 1963 attended by thousands of people. In it, he expressed hope for a future America where racial equality, brotherhood, and freedom for all would become a reality. In 1964, King was awarded a Nobel Peace Prize.

After 1965, the civil rights movement began to splinter, and its progress slowed. King thought that the movement needed a change of focus to push for more employment among African Americans. He joined with other leaders in planning a "Poor People's March" in Washington the summer of 1968. In the spring, he traveled to Memphis, Tennessee, to urge support for a strike by a group of city workers. There, on April 4, 1968, he was shot to death.

The Civil Rights Movement

Meanwhile, African Americans continued their struggle for equal rights. They made some major gains. In the early 1960s, they were active mainly in the South. (Later, the civil rights movement moved north.)

Early in 1960, black college students began a protest in Greensboro, North Carolina. They simply sat at the whites-only lunch counter of a dime store, waiting to be served. The students called their action a "sit-in." They were never served, but they hoped to win support from around the country that would force the Greensboro store, and others, to abandon segregation.

Angry whites jeered and cursed them, but the African American students returned each day and sat down again. The action spread to other stores and public places in other states. Whites and blacks marched in support of the sit-ins. Eventually, some stores ordered an end to segregated lunch counters.

In October 1960, Martin Luther King, Jr., was put in jail—along with a number of other ministers—for a sit-in in Atlanta, Georgia. The vice president, Richard Nixon, felt that it would be inappropriate to do anything. But Robert Kennedy, brother of presidential hopeful John Kennedy, contacted local officials and won King's release. That action won John Kennedy the support of many black voters in the fall election.

Over the years, however, Southern states had found ways to make it difficult for blacks to vote, depriving them of a basic right. Some imposed poll taxes, which meant anyone registering to vote had to pay a tax. Others disqualified voters who were unable to read. These restrictions were deliberately aimed at excluding Southern blacks (who were often poor and poorly-educated) from voting. The unfair laws were vigorously opposed by the civil rights movement. The Student Nonviolent Coordinating Committee (SNCC), a group of African American college students, was the main challenger of these Southern laws.

Protest Brings Violence

Once in office, Kennedy's need for the votes of Southern Democrats in Congress hampered his ability to support civil rights moves. If the president was slow or unable to act, however, African Americans were ready. In 1961, black and white students launched "Freedom Rides." The Freedom Riders traveled on buses to Southern cities hoping to force the desegregation of bus stations. At several stops, they were met by angry crowds of protesters who attacked and beat them. The president asked for a "cooling-off period," but the riders refused to stop the rides. African Americans, they said, had been cooling off too long already.

The situation grew dangerous. In Birmingham, Alabama, federal marshals and National Guard troops were needed to stop a mob from harming more than 1,500 African Americans —including Martin Luther King—meeting in a church. Robert Kennedy, now attorney general, ordered that bus stations must be integrated.

In October 1962, a federal court ordered the University of Mississippi to accept an African American, James Meredith, as a student. Kennedy sent federal troops to quiet an angry protest and protect Meredith as he registered. The following year, the focus shifted again to Birmingham, Alabama. King

Two Freedom Riders, John Lewis (left) and James Zwerg (right) stand together after being attacked by white pro-segregationists in Montgomery, Alabama, in May 1961. Pictures such as this one aroused growing support for the civil rights movement.

On August 28, 1963, the large and peaceful March on Washington took place. More than 200,000 people, white and black, marched in favor of equal rights. Here, Martin Luther King is seen waving to the huge crowd.

led a series of protests there. The police tried to end the demonstration by using police dogs, tear gas, and streams of water shot from fire hoses. Americans were shocked to see news film of children being subjected to this rough handling. The fierce attacks on the protesters won more sympathy for the civil rights movement.

Later in 1963, Alabama Governor George Wallace tried to block African American students from being enrolled in the state university. Once again, the students entered the college because of a court order. Once again, federal marshals were needed to enforce that order.

Events persuaded Kennedy to take stronger action. He announced that he would introduce in Congress a bill to ban segregation in stores, restaurants, theaters, and hotels; to end discrimination in hiring; and to move more quickly for school integration. Kennedy introduced his civil rights bill in June 1963, but it stalled in Congress.

"I have a dream that one day this nation will rise up, live out the true meaning of its creed: 'We hold these truths to be self-evident, that all men are created equal.' I have a dream that one day on the red hills of Georgia sons of former slaves and the sons of former slaveowners will be able to sit down together at the table of brotherhood. . . . I have a dream that my four little children will one day live in a nation where they will not be judged by the color of their skin but by the content of their character."

Martin Luther King, Jr., March on Washington, August 28, 1963

President and Mrs. Kennedy smile from the back of their car at the crowds lining their route in Dallas, Texas, on November 22, 1963. Just a few minutes after this picture was taken, the president was shot and killed.

"This is a sad time for all people. We have suffered a loss that cannot be weighed. I will do my best. That is all I can do. I ask for your help—and God's."

President Lyndon Johnson at the death of President Kennedy, November 23, 1963

Assassination

In late 1963, President John Kennedy took a routine political trip to Texas. He planned to make a few appearances, deliver speeches, and begin to rally the Democrats for the presidential election the next year. His wife came along, as did Vice President Lyndon Johnson and his wife. On November 22, 1963, Kennedy and his wife rode in an open-topped car in Dallas, Texas. Suddenly, shots rang out. One struck Kennedy in the head. The car's driver sped him to the hospital, but there was nothing doctors could do. The president was dead.

Johnson was sworn in as president while flying on the presidential plane back to Washington. Standing at his side was Kennedy's widow, still in the bloodstained suit she had been wearing when her husband was shot.

Americans were stunned by Kennedy's shooting. For the next three days, millions were glued to their televisions as the networks showed crowds filing past Kennedy's body lying in state, and then broadcast his funeral. People across the country—rich and poor, black and white, city dweller and farmer—joined together to grieve.

In the midst of these somber scenes, there were more shocks. First, a man named Lee Harvey Oswald was arrested and charged with the killing. A day later, he was being led through a Dallas police station to be taken to another jail. As TV cameras showed the scene live, a nightclub owner named Jack Ruby stepped from the edge of the crowd and shot Oswald dead. It was never discovered why Ruby had committed the murder.

A New President

Lyndon Johnson was a man of action, a dynamic political leader in his own right, and an experienced former senator from Texas. Johnson used all his knowledge to full advantage

in the next few months. In February 1964, he pushed, prodded, and persuaded the Senate to pass a tax cut that Kennedy had proposed.

That same month, Johnson took a bolder step. The House of Representatives had passed Kennedy's civil rights bill, and now it was moving to the Senate. Southern senators, mostly Johnson's fellow Democrats, opposed it. Johnson looked to the Republicans in the Senate for support, and finally, on June 19, the Senate passed the Civil Rights Act of 1964. It was the boldest step yet taken toward ending racial segregation and discrimination in the United States.

With the support of Republicans, but without the backing of white Southerners from his own Democratic party, President Johnson signed the Civil Rights Act on July 2, 1964.

The Great Society

Early in 1964, Johnson announced a "War on Poverty." By July, Congress approved $948 million in funding for Johnson's programs to improve employment, education, work training, and public services. Johnson said his goal was to build the "Great Society."

For the 1964 presidential election, the Republican party nominated Senator Barry Goldwater, a staunch conservative who said Johnson's plans involved too much government interference and spending. But Johnson traveled the country campaigning for the Great Society.

In November 1964, Johnson won in a landslide victory, defeating Goldwater by 16 million votes. The year after the election was very busy for Congress and victorious for the president. In nine months in 1965, Congress passed 89 bills that the Johnson administration had written or supported.

The New Legislation

One of the bills passed by Congress established the Medicare program. With this law, the government took responsibility to pay for the health care of older Americans. Johnson also

"In your time we have the opportunity to move not only toward the rich society and the powerful society, but upward to the Great Society. The Great Society rests on abundance and liberty for all. It demands an end to poverty and injustice."

President Lyndon Johnson, Ann Arbor, Michigan, May 22, 1964

won passage of a bill creating Medicaid, a similar program that benefited the poor.

Another act formed a new government department for housing and urban development. Robert Weaver was made head of the department and thus became the first African American to hold a Cabinet office. The National Endowment for the Arts and Humanities was created to fund art groups and scholars. The Elementary and Secondary Education Act offered help for education. Other laws tried to halt air and water pollution. Another made changes in the quotas, or maximum numbers, of immigrants allowed into the United States from other countries.

Johnson's programs had some success. The number of Americans living in poverty dropped from 21 percent in 1959 to 12 percent in 1969. Among African Americans, the poverty rate dropped by almost half. The elderly received health care they could not afford previously. But Johnson's vision was never fulfilled. One reason was a looming war (see Chapter 5).

The Great Society Lives On

Americans continue to argue about the benefits and disadvantages of social programs. However, the Great Society lives on. In 1965, a small effort began to offer early education to disadvantaged children. It was called the Head Start program. Decades later, Head Start still serves children across the country. It is successful, not just in giving opportunities to young children, but because it improves their chances in later life.

The greatest legacy of the Great Society, though, may be Medicare. The program grew to reach nearly 40 million Americans. But worries about the aging of the American population haunt the program. Medicare's funding comes from taxes paid by workers. As more people retire, there are fewer workers to pay those necessary taxes. Also, Americans are living longer, so the elderly receive Medicare benefits for more years. And since they often need the most expensive medical care, the costs of Medicare continue to increase. Economic experts predict that unless something is changed, the Medicare system could run out of money early in the twenty-first century.

Voices of Protest

While Kennedy and Johnson tried to push through reforms, Americans were stirring on their own. The 1960s saw a rise in political awareness as different groups began to call for an end to discrimination. Getting the most attention in the middle of the decade was the continuing struggle by African Americans.

Civil Rights Protests

African Americans achieved much in the 1950s and early 1960s. But these gains were weak, they realized, unless black people had the power of the vote. Many states, especially in the South, still had laws that made it difficult, if not impossible, for blacks to vote. Overcoming the barriers placed by these laws became a focus of the civil rights movement.

In 1964—the same summer that saw the Civil Rights Act signed into law—civil rights workers staged what they called "Freedom Summer." Thousands of protesters, black and white, traveled to the South to demonstrate against barriers to black voting and to help African Americans register to vote. Southern whites staged loud and bitter protests of their own, but the civil rights workers carried on despite the threats they received. Three of the workers disappeared. It was later found that they had been murdered.

In Mississippi, a group of Democrats committed to integration formed their own state Democratic party organization. They came to the Democratic national convention in 1964 and demanded to be seated instead of the official, pro-segregation delegates (party representatives).

"Their cause must be our cause too. Because it is not just Negroes, but really it is all of us, who must overcome the crippling legacy of bigotry and injustice. And we shall overcome."

President Lyndon Johnson, March 15, 1965

Marchers participating in a civil rights protest at Selma, Alabama, in March 1965 are met by a white man holding a Confederate flag, symbol of the pro-slavery South during the Civil War, The flag continued to be used by Southern whites to show opposition to racial equality.

"We should be peaceful, law-abiding, but the time has come for the American Negro to fight back in self-defense whenever and wherever he is being unjustly and unlawfully attacked."

Malcolm X, March 12, 1964

President Johnson didn't want to risk losing the support of Southern whites in the fall election, so he put in place a compromise that seated two pro-integration delegates but left the regular state delegates in place. Neither side was happy.

In the spring of 1965, a major protest for voting rights was staged at Selma, Alabama, followed by a march to the state capital of Montgomery. The local police cracked down on the demonstrators, beating them with clubs and throwing hundreds in jail. The protest continued, and 25,000 marchers arrived in Montgomery on March 25.

Many in the nation were becoming angry at the brutality used toward protesters. President Johnson used this growing sympathy to introduce a strong new civil rights bill. This one would guarantee voting rights for blacks. By August 6, 1965, Johnson was signing the Voting Rights Act into law.

Radical Voices

The civil rights movement was entering a difficult phase, however. Frustration at slow progress led many African Americans to make angry demands for more radical action. Leaders like King who supported nonviolent protest were losing influence. The compromise staged at the Democratic national convention in 1964 left many blacks embittered.

One voice for more radical action was that of Malcolm X. He was a member of the Nation of Islam, a church formed by African Americans who were Muslims. Malcolm X believed that whites would only grant equality to African Americans under pressure, and he rejected the policy of nonviolence. Malcolm X's call for violent action appealed to many blacks.

Malcolm X (1925–65)

Malcolm X , born Malcolm Little in Omaha, Nebraska, had a troubled childhood. His family's house was burned down by the Ku Klux Klan, a white racist group, and his father was murdered when Malcolm was only six. His mother had a mental breakdown and was put in an institution. Malcolm fell into street crime and, in 1946, he was convicted of burglary and sent to prison.

His life changed when he entered the religious group Nation of Islam while in prison. After his release, he took the name Malcolm X. The "X" signified that his family had lost its name because it had to take the name of white slaveholders.

Malcolm X became a brilliant spokesman for the Black Power movement. In New York City, he preached against integration and for black separatism and black pride. In 1964, because of disagreements with its leaders, Malcolm X broke with the Nation of Islam to form his own group, the Organization of Afro-American Unity (OAAU). The two groups immediately entered into a feud.

Malcolm X speaking in Harlem, New York City, in 1963.

That same year, Malcolm X went on a pilgrimage to Mecca, a Muslim holy place in Saudi Arabia. There, he became convinced by the Muslim message of the brotherhood of all people. When Malcolm X returned to the United States, he began to speak of blacks and whites working together. He was killed early in 1965, possibly by agents of the Nation of Islam, the group that Malcolm X had rejected.

49

Some members of the Student Nonviolent Coordinating Committee (SNCC) were also feeling frustrated. In 1966, impatient with the slow pace of change, members of SNCC began to speak of "Black Power." This term described the radical movement growing among African Americans, and the phrase caused alarm among some whites.

Another problem surfaced as well. Hundreds of thousands of African Americans lived in cities in the North and West. Many lived in slums that were marked by poverty because white racism denied them equal access to housing and to jobs. African Americans were segregated from whites in education, not by law, but because they attended schools in their own poor, black neighborhoods. They also faced increasingly poor relations with the city police.

Violence Erupts

These factors produced anger and frustration that boiled over several times in riots. In 1964, the police shooting of an African American led to a riot in New York City's Harlem, a black neighborhood. The following year, a simple traffic arrest led to an explosion of rage in Watts, a section of Los Angeles. Summer after summer, the nation waited to see which city would next erupt in violence. The riots generated fear in the white community, where many people began to feel that the push for rights was becoming dangerous.

The federal government took some steps to try to solve the problems underlying the riots. Courts ordered Northern school systems to enforce integration, even if it meant taking children to schools outside of their own neighborhoods. And Johnson urged employers to take affirmative action (see page 56) to bring more blacks into the workforce.

Native American Rights

The black civil rights movement inspired other groups. More than 400 Native American leaders met in Chicago in 1961 in an attempt to find ways of improving the lives of Indians. The meeting issued a statement called the Declaration of

Indian Purpose that called for "the right to choose our own way of life" and "preserving our precious heritage."

From this meeting flowed a growing Indian activism and cooperation among different tribes. Indians received some support from new federal laws. In 1968, Congress extended provisions of some of the War on Poverty programs to include Native Americans. That same year, the Indian Civil Rights Act guaranteed protection by the Bill of Rights to all Native Americans. The law also said that, on the reservations, tribal laws would be in force.

A growing number of young Indians felt that this progress was too little, too late. In 1969, a group called the American Indian Movement (AIM) seized Alcatraz Island in San Francisco Bay to symbolize the seizure of Indian land. In 1973, a group of AIM members took control of Wounded Knee, part of the Sioux reservation in South Dakota. Neither of these actions did much to help improve Native American rights. Indians had more success with actions in the courts. In several cases, federal judges ruled that Indians had to be given land to fulfill treaty obligations from earlier centuries. In other rulings, Indians won the right to control the use of valuable resources on their land.

Members of AIM stand guard during their protest occupation of Wounded Knee on the Sioux reservation in South Dakota on March 7, 1973. Wounded Knee was the site of a massacre of Indians by the U.S. Army in 1890.

La Raza Unida

Hispanic Americans, too, were growing restive. One barrier to strong Hispanic political action was that Hispanics belonged to many communities, not just one. The group included Mexicans, who lived mainly in the states from Texas to California; Puerto Ricans, who lived mostly in the cities of the Northeast; and Cubans, concentrated in New Jersey and Florida. Each group, while sharing a common language, had its own culture.

Cesar Chavez (1927–93)

For decades, many Mexican Americans moved from farm to farm in California, Texas, and other states. They were migrant workers, moving with the harvest to pick crops for farmers as they became ripe. The work was backbreaking and the hours long. Migrant workers began laboring as children and were paid pennies.

Cesar Chavez (left, in checked shirt) with a group of striking agricultural workers in Delano, California, in 1967.

Cesar Chavez grew up as a migrant worker. In his twenties, he began to work for voting rights for Hispanics. Chavez founded the United Farm Workers (UFW), a union for agricultural workers. In 1965, the UFW staged a strike against grape growers. Chavez used the tactics of nonviolent protest. He led marches, campaigned in the press, and went on hunger strikes. Chavez convinced many Americans to help by refusing to buy produce in stores. This public support of the UFW forced farmers to recognize the union. They granted better wages and several other benefits.

Some conditions improved, but growers used the threat of hiring non-union workers to prevent the union from becoming too powerful. Still, Chavez had made an impact and his movement affected more than just migrant workers. It renewed Hispanic Americans' pride in their culture and launched a new wave of activism among Hispanics.

One remarkable Hispanic effort was that of a group of migrant workers led by Cesar Chavez, who in 1963 founded the National Farm Workers Association. This labor union later became the United Farm Workers. Mexican Americans also gained some political success in the Southwest and California, starting with the 1969 formation of a political party called *La Raza Unida*, meaning "the united people."

The Feminist Movement

Another struggle for equality was emerging among America's women. During World War II, women had broken out of their traditional role as homemakers when thousands of men went overseas to fight. They had entered the workforce to fill the gaps left by enlisted men, and had played a major part in producing materials for the war effort. When the war ended and men returned, many women in the mid-1940s returned to work inside the home, as they had done in earlier times.

However, the seeds of dissatisfaction had been sown. In the early 1960s, growing numbers of women began to fight for acceptance in the workplace and equal opportunities. In 1963, Congress passed a law aimed at ending a longstanding problem: the fact that women were paid less than men who had the same job. The Equal Pay Act barred this practice. The following year, Congress acted again. The Civil Rights Act of 1964 applied all the provisions of the law to women.

Feminists, feeling the government was not doing enough, took action themselves. Feminist leaders joined together to form a new political group, the National Organization for Women (NOW). The group campaigned for "equality of opportunity and freedom of choice" for women.

The women's movement did affect some social change: Colleges that had been all-male chose to admit women, and some women's schools began to admit men. Many colleges opened departments of women's studies. More women began to enter law and medicine. Business began to feel the effects of a growing percentage of working women, and by the mid-1970s, more than half of all married women worked.

Betty Friedan (b. 1921)

Betty Friedan was born in Peoria, Illinois. After attending Smith College, she married and became a housewife. During the 1950s, Friedan lived in a lovely house in a New York suburb with a good husband and wonderful children. Everything was perfect, according to the values of the 1950s. But for Friedan, something was missing, and she realized that many other women felt the same. She wrote her conclusions in *The Feminine Mystique*. In the book, Friedan argued that college-educated women felt frustrated by being forced to abandon their careers in favor of raising families. A question nagged within them, Friedan said —"Is that all there is?" Critics attacked Friedan's ideas, but the book gave a voice to thousands of women.

Friedan served as president of the National Organization of Women until 1970 and remained active in the women's movement during the 1970s. She raised a new storm of protest—this time among feminists—with her 1981 book *The Second Stage*. In it, Friedan warned against the new focus on women having careers at the expense of their families. In 1993, Friedan published *The Fountain of Age*, about the place in society held by older people.

Extremism and Opposition

Some young feminists began to take more extreme positions. They said that men systematically exploited women, and they even spoke out against marriage. Because this extremism was identified with feminism, NOW was opposed by more conservative women who may otherwise have agreed with such demands as equal pay for equal work. Other women refused to join the feminist movement because they felt that the sexes were different and ought to be treated differently. Some women who were homemakers were insulted by the feminist claim that caring for a home and family was boring and unfulfilling. As a result, there was opposition to women's rights, just as there was to civil rights for minorities.

One other minority caused concern when it began to assert its rights. In the late 1960s, homosexuals took an increasingly public position, demanding an end to the denial of their rights and to abuse by others. Homosexuals began to call themselves "gay" and loudly proclaimed "Gay Pride." Some Americans agreed that citizens should not be punished for being gay. Many others opposed this outspoken behavior from a group they considered to be morally wrong.

The Counterculture

Another protest movement arose, this one among America's young. Inspired by the Beats of the 1950s and by the rebellious lyrics of rock and roll, teens and young adults began to reject mainstream American values. Their protest came to be called "the counterculture."

Members of the counterculture called themselves "hippies," wore ragged jeans and multi-colored flowing clothes, and grew their hair long to signal their lack of concern for mainstream appearance. Hippies preached peace and love, and many traveled to the Haight-Ashbury district of San Francisco, where they proclaimed a "Summer of Love" in 1967. Their philosophy led hippies to a heightened interest in mysticism and Eastern philosophy. Ideas about the oneness of all creation appealed to youthful idealists, with their belief in equality and rejection of consumer values.

Another aspect of the counterculture was the increasing use of mind-altering drugs. The number of people who

In the summer of 1967, a hippie girl stands next to her camper van in San Francisco. Thousands of young people flocked to the city in the "Summer of Love," seeking music, drugs, and fellow members of the counterculture movement.

"We are the people of this generation, bred in at least moderate comfort, housed in universities, looking uncomfortably to the world we inherit."

Students for a Democratic Society, in a statement calling for radical changes in American society, 1962

smoked marijuana increased. LSD, a drug that dramatically changed perceptions, became popular. Rock and roll helped fuel the rising popularity of drug use. Drug overdoses became a tragic side-effect of the counterculture.

Mainstream American values, particularly political values, were rejected by critics called the "New Left." (Liberal beliefs are often called "left-wing," whereas conservative views are termed "right-wing.") The young people of the New Left were appalled by the racism they saw confronting the civil rights movement. They protested the government's use of military power around the world. They also objected to America's acceptance of dictators in non-communist nations who oppressed their citizens. They sympathized with the poor in Asia and Africa who, they said, might benefit from the equality promised under communism. Most of all, the New Left challenged American involvement in Vietnam.

Affirmative Action

In 1965, President Johnson urged that companies that did work for the federal government should take "affirmative action" to hire more women and minorities. In 1972, the Equal Employment Opportunity Act was passed. The new law said that decisions about hiring and job advancement should be made without regard to sex or race. Until that ideal was reached, employers had to take positive steps to increase the number of women and minorities they hired.

The idea was controversial from the start. Most people accepted the goal of sex-blind and race-blind hiring. But critics attacked the affirmative action programs that aimed to increase the proportion of women and minority employees. They charged that setting aside a certain proportion of jobs or school places for females or minorities was "reverse discrimination." That is, white males were being penalized because they were not female or members of a minority group.

The debate went on for years. In the 1990s, the Supreme Court made several decisions that put limits on affirmative action. These decisions did not declare the practice unconstitutional, however.

Vietnam

John Kennedy and Lyndon Johnson had both served in Congress in the early years of the Cold War. There, they developed a mistrust of the Soviet Union and a tendency to read Soviet aggression into local conflicts around the world. They had seen Truman, a Democratic president, weakened when communists took control of China. Kennedy and Johnson were convinced of the superiority of American weaponry and eager to assert American power. It is hardly surprising that, as presidents, they led the United States into war in Vietnam.

The Situation in Vietnam

Before World War II, Vietnam was part of the French colonial empire. During that war, Japan expelled the French. When the war ended in 1945, the French tried to return. The Vietnamese leader Ho Chi Minh, who was a nationalist, began a war to keep them out. Americans were sympathetic to nationalist causes, and Ho Chi Minh appealed to the American government for help. However, along with being a nationalist, Ho was a devoted communist. The Truman administration, therefore, refused to support him.

The French struggle to regain control of Vietnam dragged on for nine years, into the 1950s. During this period, both Truman and then Eisenhower supported the French with money and weapons. If Vietnam were to fall to communism, they feared, neighboring nations would too. This was known as the "domino" theory.

By 1954, Ho Chi Minh's forces had won control of much of the country, and several of Eisenhower's advisers urged him to use the American military to rescue the French. The president refused, and the last major French force in Vietnam surrendered in spring 1954. In July 1954, at a conference in Geneva, Switzerland, the French and Ho Chi Minh signed a peace plan called the Geneva Agreements. As had happened in Korea, Vietnam was temporarily divided into northern and southern halves. Ho Chi Minh would rule in the North; a pro-Western regime would control the South. Elections were promised for 1956, when the Vietnamese people would choose one leader for the whole nation.

America Gets Involved

Eisenhower immediately threw American support behind Ngo Dinh Diem, who led South Vietnam. The Americans also discouraged Diem from pursuing the promised elections. This was because they were convinced that Ho Chi Minh's wide support would give him an easy victory and produce a communist Vietnam. As a result, in October 1955, Diem announced that South Vietnam was an independent republic and he was its president.

Diem was not an ideal ally. He refused to make changes to help Vietnam's poor, and he and his government were corrupt. This increased popular resentment of his rule. Diem was also a member of Vietnam's Catholic minority. He roused popular anger by taking steps to weaken Buddhism, the faith followed by most Vietnamese.

Rebels against Diem in South Vietnam received aid from Ho's government in the North. By 1960, a group called the National Front for the Liberation of Vietnam, or the Viet Cong, had organized in the South and was fighting against government forces. As the situation in the South worsened, Eisenhower supplied more and more aid. By the end of his term as president, 650 Americans served in Vietnam as military advisers. Their mission was to train the South Vietnamese to fight and win the civil war being waged.

When John Kennedy became president in 1961, he brought a new approach to intervention in foreign conflicts. He and his advisers believed that Eisenhower's policy of massive retaliation (see page 18) would not work if it was

tried in Vietnam. Instead, they thought the United States needed to follow a policy of "flexible response." They wanted to have small, lightly-armed, mobile army units that could fight in the poor nations of Latin America, Africa, and Asia. Vietnam seemed an ideal place to try out this flexible response policy.

But by 1963, the Viet Cong seemed to be winning in Vietnam, and Diem's moves against Buddhists had caused widespread protest. With Kennedy's agreement, a group of South Vietnam's military officers overthrew Diem and took control of the government. Not long afterward, Kennedy was assassinated, and Vietnam became Lyndon Johnson's problem.

Johnson Sends More Troops

President Johnson had little experience in foreign affairs or defense matters. He moved cautiously at first, sending only a few thousand more advisers. He was not eager to commit American troops to a growing war.

Then, in August 1964, American destroyers and North Vietnamese gunboats clashed in the Gulf of Tonkin, off North Vietnam. The exact details of what happened are unclear, but Johnson saw the incident as a challenge to American power. The gunboats attacked the destroyers in international waters, he said, and he asked Congress to

During President Kennedy's administration, American troop strength in Vietnam jumped to 15,500. By 1968, hundreds of thousands of Americans, crowded onto ships and airplanes, had left home to enter the war in Vietnam.

Lyndon Baines Johnson (1908–73)

When Lyndon Johnson was 12, he told classmates that he would be president one day. Following a childhood of poverty in the tough Texas hill country, Johnson trained and worked as a teacher. He first went to Washington in 1932 as an aide to a Texas representative.

President Johnson preparing a public address on the Vietnam War.

Johnson won election to Congress in 1937. There, he came under the wing of fellow Texan Sam Rayburn, Speaker of the House. Rayburn helped Johnson get ahead and taught him how to lead. Johnson used those lessons after reaching the Senate in 1948.

Johnson tried to gain the Democratic nomination for president in 1960 but lost to Kennedy. Many were surprised when he accepted the vice presidency, as Johnson enjoyed power and would have had more of it by staying in the Senate. For over three years, he served as vice president, resenting his lack of responsibility and the lack of respect he received from the president's advisers.

Johnson was a complex man. He was a quick thinker with a superb memory, but he had an unpolished manner. Always remembering his own beginnings, Johnson strove to better the lives of the disadvantaged. Eager for praise, he was stung by mounting criticism of him and his administration. Johnson had achieved great triumphs, but he left the presidency in sadness and disappointment. An energetic and passionate man when he became president, he was forced by a heart condition to live quietly in retirement.

authorize a tough response. With no opposing votes in the House and only two in the Senate, Congress passed the Gulf of Tonkin Resolution. It allowed Johnson to "take all necessary measures" in Vietnam. Critics later said that Congress had given Johnson a blank check to conduct the war.

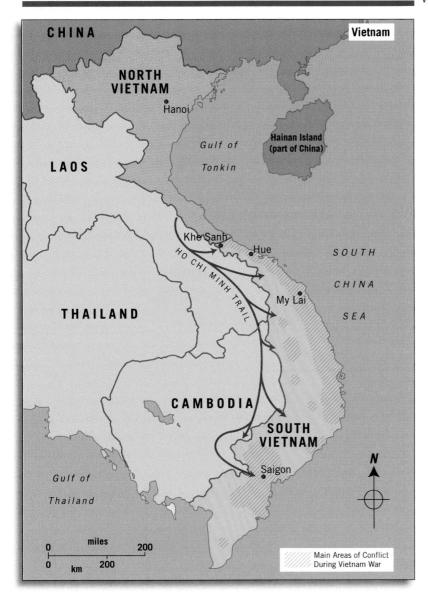

CHINA

Vietnam

NORTH
VIETNAM

Hanoi

Gulf of

Hainan Island
(part of China)

LAOS

Tonkin

Khe Sanh

Hue

SOUTH

HO CHI MINH TRAIL

CHINA

THAILAND

My Lai

SEA

CAMBODIA

SOUTH
VIETNAM

N

Saigon

Gulf of

Thailand

miles

0   200

0   200
km

Main Areas of Conflict
During Vietnam War

This map shows the areas in Vietnam where conflict was prolonged over several years. In Laos and Cambodia, the Ho Chi Minh Trail offered a route for communist soldiers coming from North Vietnam to fight South Vietnamese and American troops south of the border.

Early in 1965, seven U.S. Marines were killed in a Viet Cong attack on an American base. Johnson struck back. He ordered American planes to drop bombs on North Vietnam in an effort to punish the North and halt the flow of soldiers and supplies that came south along the Ho Chi Minh Trail. This was a route that led from North Vietnam to South Vietnam through the jungles of neighboring Laos and Cambodia. The American bombing continued for several years.

Johnson also began to increase sharply the number of American troops serving in Vietnam. There were 180,000 at the end of 1965, and more than twice as many by the end of 1966. By 1968, the number had grown to more than 500,000. In the summer of 1965, Johnson had announced that the U.S. troops would take offensive actions against the Viet Cong and the North Vietnamese army. Vietnam had become America's war.

Johnson's commitment of more troops had another effect. The rising cost of the war forced him to ask for a tax increase in 1967. He won it only by agreeing to cut $6 billion from the budget for Great Society programs.

Fighting in Vietnam

America had far more military might than the Viet Cong and the North Vietnamese army. But its large tanks and artillery were of little use in the thick jungles, hills, and rice paddies of Vietnam. The guerrilla forces opposed to the Americans thrived in this environment. They could move quietly, hidden by the vegetation, and then strike quickly and without warning. The Vietnamese startled American soldiers in the night with quick, fierce attacks of gunfire, known as fire fights, and just as quickly stole away. The stunned Americans were left to tend to their dead and wounded, and wonder when and where the next strike would come.

American soldiers set fire to a Vietnamese village in 1967. In the remote areas of South Vietnam, U.S. troops had learned to be suspicious of apparently innocent villagers who may have been Viet Cong supporters, ready to kill Americans at any moment.

My Lai

Sometimes the extremes of stress suffered by American soldiers in Vietnam erupted into terrible war crimes. The My Lai massacre stands as the worst example. In March 1968, Lieutenant William Calley led his platoon into My Lai, a small community that was part of Song My village in Vietnam's Quangtri Province. Although the soldiers found no Viet Cong, Calley had all the people of My Lai assembled. Then he ordered his men to kill every single Vietnamese: mostly old men, women, and children. It is estimated that between 175 and 200 My Lai residents were killed, and at least another 250 civilians were massacred in the immediate area.

News of the massacre did not reach the United States until 1969. When it did, Americans were outraged. The action undermined the claim that American soldiers were fighting for justice and honor, and the result was increased support for the growing antiwar movement. In a military court-martial that lasted from late 1970 to early 1971, Calley was found guilty of murder and sentenced to prison. He was the only member of the army who was punished for My Lai.

The Viet Cong and North Vietnamese controlled the small villages in rural South Vietnam. Villagers often sympathized with these forces, giving soldiers food and information about American troop movements. When they entered villages, American soldiers found it difficult to tell who was an enemy and who a friend. Errors led to deaths in both directions. Some soldiers were killed by villagers who hid weapons and then ambushed them. Soldiers sometimes killed innocent villagers, including women and children, out of fear and mistrust.

Over the years, morale among American troops plunged. The tension of walking among land mines, being ambushed, and facing the unknown became unbearable for many soldiers.

The Soldiers

Most soldiers fighting in Vietnam were draftees, meaning they were required by law to enter the military if they were

"When we marched into the rice paddies . . . we carried, along with our packs and rifles, the implicit convictions that the Vietcong could be quickly beaten. We kept the packs and rifles; the convictions, we lost."

Philip Caputo, A Rumor of War, 1977

American soldiers drafted into the armed forces during the Vietnam War were mostly young, inexperienced, and poor. They were fighting many miles from home in a war that often seemed as senseless as it was brutal. Many thousands never fully recovered from the experience, even if they survived the warfare.

chosen. Others, mostly from higher-income families, found ways to avoid service, such as leaving the country or going to college. (Full-time students could be excused from the draft while in college.) As a result, the soldiers in Vietnam were predominantly from the poorer segments of society. African Americans made up 20 percent, even though only 10 percent of the nation's population was black. This overrepresentation of African Americans was one of the reasons that civil rights leaders like Martin Luther King, Jr., criticized the war.

The soldiers, drafted at age 18, came from the same age group that was experimenting with drugs back in the United States. Soon, drug use became widespread among American soldiers serving in Vietnam. Drugs provided escape from the grind and torment of the war and eased the pain of the death of close friends. Growing drug use, combined with little preparation and training for war, undermined the soldiers' ability to fight effectively.

Strategy and Loss of Life

Morale also suffered due to the conduct of the war itself. The South Vietnamese villagers that Americans were supposed to be saving often suffered in attacks on the ground and from the air. To clear villages of Viet Cong fighters, American troops sometimes torched them. One American commander's comment on this strategy became an ironic commentary on the war. "We had to destroy the town," he said, "in order to save it." Soldiers wondered whether their lives were being put on the line for any purpose.

The war witnessed by soldiers on the ground was not the war that top military officials saw. Officials in American headquarters issued weekly body counts that compared mounting American losses to even higher losses among the North Vietnamese. Over time, many Americans came to mistrust these counts. American officials, however, spoke optimistically. Secretary of Defense Robert McNamara said he could see "the light at the end of the tunnel."

Protesting the War

Despite this, a growing number of people at home noted that ever larger numbers of soldiers, equipment, and dollars were being funneled to Vietnam. They read about growing protests by the people of South Vietnam. They watched news reports on television of young soldiers caught in guerrilla attacks. They saw hundreds of American soldiers coming home in body bags. President Johnson was caught in what was called a "credibility gap." Fewer and fewer Americans believed what he said.

An antiwar movement had started back in 1965, when several colleges staged "teach-ins" to explore issues raised by the war. In the spring of that year, antiwar leaders organized a march in Washington that brought together 20,000 protesters.

Connected to the antiwar movement was a protest against the draft. The draft scared many young men. When President Johnson announced changes in 1966 that made it harder to avoid the draft by going to college, loud protests rang out on campuses across the country. Thousands avoided the draft by leaving the country for Canada or Sweden. Protesters began to burn their draft cards, the papers that showed that they were registered.

More conservative Americans thought that these actions smacked of disloyalty. The nation increasingly became divided into "doves," who wanted an end to the war, and "hawks," who believed that the United States should continue to fight. Antiwar marches were often matched by demonstrations against the marchers.

In 1967, about 75,000 protesters gathered at an antiwar rally in Washington, D.C. Carrying signs painted with antiwar and anti-draft slogans, they marched to the Pentagon—center of the Defense Department—where they were met with tear gas.

In 1966, Senator William J. Fulbright of Arkansas gave support to those who argued against the war. As chairman of the Senate Foreign Relations Committee, he held hearings in which prominent Americans explained why they viewed Vietnam as the wrong place for a fight. In 1967, though, the vast majority of Americans still supported the war. In one poll, two-thirds of the people who gave their opinion thought that the United States was right to fight. Half believed that stronger attacks against North Vietnam would win the war, and 70 percent questioned the loyalty of the people who protested against the war.

Weapons of War

The American effort in Vietnam included powerful weapons. During the massive air attacks on the North, 6.2 million tons (5.6 million metric tons) of bombs were dropped. This was more than twice the number of bombs dropped by Americans in World War I, World War II, and the Korean War combined.

Some of those bombs contained napalm. This highly flammable combination of chemicals set large areas of the countryside instantly on fire. Ground soldiers used flame throwers armed with napalm to burn villages. The United States Army also sprayed the countryside with herbicides, or chemicals that kill vegetation. The aim was to destroy the jungle greenery that gave cover to the Viet Cong guerrillas. Many Vietnam veterans claimed that Agent Orange, a lethal herbicide, had a devastating effect on them. They pointed to ailments they suffered later and birth defects that affected their children. Long after the war ended, Congress passed a bill giving these veterans extra health benefits.

Vietnamese citizens flee from a napalm attack, carrying two severely wounded infants.

The End of the War

A s the United States entered 1968, war continued in Southeast Asia, and tension rose at home. It was an election year, and the vote was expected to be the people's judgment on the Vietnam War. But the year held several surprises.

The Tet Offensive

On January 30, 1968, the people of South Vietnam celebrated Tet, their New Year. The next day, Viet Cong and North Vietnamese units staged a huge offensive all across South Vietnam. They attacked a hundred cities and towns, and 20,000 troops struck the large U.S. Marine base at Khe Sanh. Other units captured the ancient city of Hue. Attackers even entered the American embassy in the South Vietnamese capital of Saigon and killed five people there. This many-pronged attack was called the Tet Offensive.

During the Tet Offensive of January 1968, the Viet Cong attacked several points in the city of Saigon, South Vietnam. These American troops were still fighting to regain control of North Saigon in May 1968.

American and South Vietnamese troops fought back. They regained control of Saigon and ousted the enemy from cities across the South. While it took many weeks, reinforcements drove back the attackers at Khe Sanh as well. The North Vietnamese lost more than 30,000 soldiers. The Americans and South Vietnamese lost 3,000. The North Vietnamese were unable to hold any of the positions they had taken, and the United States announced complete victory.

Public Opinion and Policy Changes

Senator George Aiken of Vermont had a different view. "If this is failure," he said, "I hope the Viet Cong never have a major success." The Tet Offensive had shaken American confidence. Before the attacks, hawks outnumbered doves by two to one. After Tet, the two sides were even, and there was a growing feeling that the war could not be won.

When opinion polls asked what people thought of the president, Johnson's approval ratings had plunged. By the end of February 1968, almost 60 percent of Americans opposed Johnson's handling of the war. The impact became clear the following month. Senator Eugene McCarthy was running against Johnson to become the Democratic party candidate for president. McCarthy was strongly antiwar. In March 1968, he pulled a huge number of votes in the first primary.

On March 31, Johnson addressed the nation on television. He announced a dramatic change in policy in Vietnam: The United States would seek a peaceful solution through negotiations. In the meantime, it would work to make the army of South Vietnam more active in fighting the war. Before closing, Johnson stunned Americans by saying that he would not run for reelection.

Soon after, Robert Kennedy—brother of the assassinated president—entered the race for the Democratic nomination. Like McCarthy, he opposed the Vietnam War. Johnson's supporters in the party lined up behind Vice President Hubert Humphrey instead.

"[The Viet Cong's] well-laid plans went afoul. . . . The enemy exposed himself by virtue of his strategy, and he suffered heavy casualties."

General William Westmoreland, 1968, after U.S. victories following the Tet Offensive

"I have concluded that I should not permit the presidency to become involved in the partisan divisions that are developing in this political year. . . . Accordingly, I shall not seek, and I will not accept, the nomination of any party for another term as your president."

President Lyndon Johnson, televised address to the nation, March 31, 1968

Two Assassinations

While the Democratic race was heating up, the nation had another shock. On April 4, 1968, Martin Luther King, Jr., was shot and killed in Memphis, Tennessee. Riots rocked many of the nation's cities in the aftermath of the King slaying. Tens of thousands of people poured into Atlanta to pay their respects at the civil rights leader's funeral, and millions watched it on television.

The Democratic presidential campaign ground on. Robert Kennedy won most of the next primaries, and antiwar forces thought they had an opportunity to capture the presidency. But on the night of his victory in the California primary, June 5, 1968, Kennedy was shot. He died the next day. The King and Kennedy slayings seemed to signal that the United States was spinning out of control.

On August 26, the Democrats gathered at a convention in Chicago to nominate a candidate for president. The antiwar forces were behind McCarthy, but without Kennedy there was little hope for victory. Humphrey won the nomination.

About 10,000 antiwar protesters came to Chicago as well. Waiting for them were the city police, led by Mayor Richard Daley. As the convention nominated Humphrey, police clashed with demonstrators. They waded into the crowd, wielding clubs and smashing down on the protesters. While the fight was going on, the protesters chanted, "The whole world is watching!" They were right. News cameras recorded the chaos and broadcast it to millions. The Democratic party seemed hopelessly split.

Nixon and Wallace

The Republican convention had also taken place in August. The easy winner was Richard Nixon, former vice president. Nixon appealed to voters who wanted an end to the turmoil they were seeing in American society. Nixon called these Americans the "silent majority."

> "We had already glimpsed the most compassionate leaders our nation could produce, and they had all been assassinated. And from this time forward, things would get worse."
>
> *Jack Newfield, Kennedy speechwriter, writing about the assassinations of the 1960s*

Delegates at the 1968 Democratic national convention in Chicago protest their own party's policy on the Vietnam War. Protests also raged outside as thousands of antiwar demonstrators converged on the convention.

Richard Nixon (1913–94)

Republican candidate Richard Nixon (center) during his 1968 presidential campaign.

Born in southern California, Richard Nixon graduated from a local college and went to Duke University Law School. He returned to California to practice law and joined the U.S. Navy when World War II began.

Soon after the war, local Republicans invited Nixon to run for Congress. After a fierce campaign, voters swept him into office. In the House of Representatives, Nixon gained fame by pursuing the alleged spy Alger Hiss. His tough anticommunism won him a Senate seat in 1950. Then he was named as Dwight Eisenhower's running mate in 1952. Nixon was almost dropped from the ticket over charges of corruption. But he gave a televised speech that won his party's support, and Eisenhower kept the young senator on.

For eight years, Nixon served as vice president, gaining experience in foreign affairs and sharply attacking Democrats. His close defeat by John Kennedy in the 1960 presidential race left him bitter. When he lost a campaign for governor of California two years later, Nixon said he was leaving politics.

By 1968, however, Nixon was back, and the Republicans gave him their presidential nomination. When he reached office, he showed signs of good statesmanship and brilliance in foreign policy. Nixon also relentlessly pursued his enemies, sometimes breaking the law in the effort. These actions led to his downfall in the Watergate scandal, and he resigned as president in 1974. Nixon was both one of the most hated and most admired of politicians in the late 1900s. He spent his retirement years writing and advising about politics.

He promised to restore "law and order." The Supreme Court had come under intense criticism for decisions that seemed too generous to criminals. Nixon said he would appoint a tough attorney general—the chief law officer of the nation—who would crack down on crime.

Nixon benefited from splits in the Democratic party. Humphrey not only had trouble from antiwar liberals, but he was challenged on the conservative right as well. George Wallace, governor of Alabama, had left the Democrats to form a third political party: the American Independent party.

In the early 1960s, Wallace had won national fame as a segregationist. By 1968, Wallace had attracted white Southerners who resented the civil rights movement. He also won support from voters who lived in Northern cities, many of them union members. They tended to be hawks on the war, but they were also attracted to Wallace's criticisms of government interference in people's lives.

During the Cold War years, voter support in the United States shifted dramatically. A Democratic nation during and after World War II turned Republican in the 1950s. By 1964, the political landscape had changed again. But voters became disillusioned with the Democrats during the Vietnam War. In 1972, the Republicans took every state except Massachusetts.

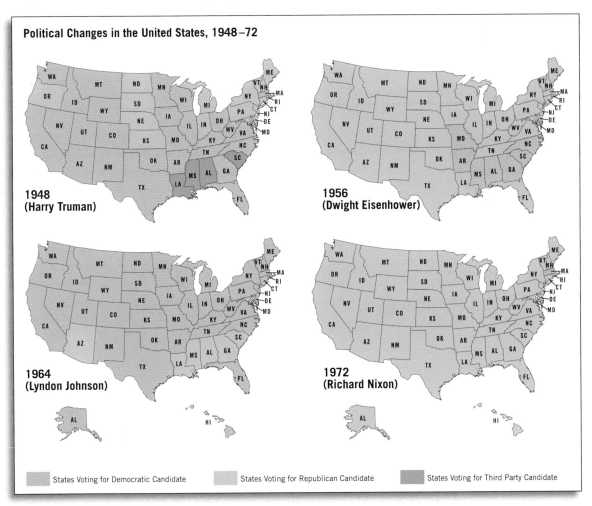

Political Changes in the United States, 1948–72

1948
(Harry Truman)

1956
(Dwight Eisenhower)

1964
(Lyndon Johnson)

1972
(Richard Nixon)

☐ States Voting for Democratic Candidate   ☐ States Voting for Republican Candidate   ☐ States Voting for Third Party Candidate

71

The big issue was the war. Nixon said he had a secret plan to end the war but would not reveal it to avoid endangering peace talks. Humphrey ran a vigorous campaign, and in October, he gained in the opinion polls when he said he would halt the bombing. In the end, it was one of the closest presidential votes in history. Wallace captured 13.5 percent of the popular vote, and Nixon defeated Humphrey by just over 500,000 votes to win the presidential election.

Nixon's War

Nixon had bold plans for American foreign policy, but first he had to find an end to the war in Vietnam. Doing so would help not only at home but also abroad, where protest against American involvement was still growing. Nixon felt that simply pulling out of Vietnam would weaken the United States. The goal, he said, was "peace with honor." He and National Security Adviser Henry Kissinger took four steps.

In May 1969, to reduce protests, they replaced the draft with a lottery system. Each 19-year-old would be assigned a number based on his birthday. Only those with the lowest numbers were likely to be called for service in Vietnam.

Next, Nixon announced in June 1969 that he was withdrawing 25,000 American troops from Vietnam. The withdrawals were part of the plan for "Vietnamization," or having South Vietnam take more responsibility for the war. The troop pullouts continued for three years. By 1972, the number of American troops in Vietnam had been drastically cut from more than 500,000 to about 60,000.

In the third step, Kissinger negotiated in France with Le Duc Tho, who represented North Vietnam. The talks made little progress, however. The major sticking point was the American insistence that North Vietnamese troops withdraw from the South before the last American troops left.

Cambodia

Nixon also pursued a get-tough policy. His fourth step was secretly to order the air force to bomb Cambodia. That nation was a neutral neighbor of Vietnam, but North Vietnamese troops used its jungles to move south. In April 1970, Nixon announced that American troops would cross the border into Cambodia to attack North Vietnamese bases there.

The antiwar movement had lost some steam in 1969 due to the changes in the draft and the troop withdrawals. The invasion of Cambodia launched a huge protest, however. Hundreds of thousands marched in Washington, D.C., and across the country. More than 1,000 college campuses were shut down by student strikes. At Kent State University in Ohio, National Guard troops brought in to maintain order fired at a crowd of students, killing four. Ten days later, an incident left two dead at Jackson State College in Mississippi.

Congress protested, voting in late 1970 to repeal, or overturn, the Gulf of Tonkin Resolution. This 1964 act had been seen as the legal justification for using armed forces in Vietnam. Despite its repeal, Nixon pursued the war.

The Pentagon Papers

In June 1971, *The New York Times* and other newspapers began to publish documents taken from government files. They had been prepared before Nixon had become president.

The Pentagon Papers showed the existence of plans to increase United States involvement in the Vietnam War well before they were made public. They also showed that some of Lyndon Johnson's top advisers had argued against the massive bombing of the North. Finally, the papers revealed that government officials had often made decisions even though they were not well informed. Given the cost of the war in American lives, this fact disturbed many people.

Although they did not reflect actions during Nixon's presidency, the Pentagon Papers helped weaken American confidence in the government. Their publication was just one of many incidents in which secret government documents appeared in the press. Nixon was outraged by these leaks. In 1971, he set up the Special Investigations Unit in the White House. The group called itself "the Plumbers" because its task was to stop leaks.

Relations with China and the Soviet Union

Nixon and Kissinger were making other foreign policy moves. Nixon wanted more stability in the world. He believed that, to achieve this, he had to ease tensions with the Soviet Union and end the isolation of communist China. Since the communist takeover there in 1949, the United States and China had had no diplomatic relations with each other. China and the Soviet Union were now rivals for power in Asia, and Nixon calculated that improved U.S.-Chinese relations would put pressure on the Soviets to be more friendly.

Kissinger made several secret trips to meet with Chinese leaders. Enough progress was made that Nixon announced he would travel to China. His trip in February 1972 was a public relations triumph. Nixon and China's Mao Zedong chatted and toasted each other at state dinners. Excursions to Chinese sites like the Great Wall were beamed back to the United States on TV. In the meantime, the United States allowed the People's Republic of China to take a seat in the United Nations. The Republic of China (see pages 13–14), led by Chiang Kai-shek, had its seat taken away.

During his successful visit to China in 1972, President Nixon (front right) inspected an impressive display of Chinese military troops. He was accompanied by Chinese Premier Zhou Enlai (front left).

President Nixon took another trip in 1972: to the Soviet Union. The policy over China had apparently paid off. The Soviets and Americans finally reached agreement on the Strategic Arms Limitation Treaty (SALT). The treaty did not actually reduce the nuclear weapons either country held. The superpowers did, however, agree to not build any more nuclear missiles of a certain type.

Henry Kissinger (b. 1923)

Henry Kissinger's family moved from Germany to the United States in the 1930s to escape the German persecution of Jews. Kissinger served in army intelligence during World War II. After the war, he became an expert in foreign and defense policy.

When Richard Nixon was elected president in 1968, he chose Kissinger as his national security adviser. The two worked closely on efforts to negotiate an end to the Vietnam War. Meanwhile, Nixon and Kissinger were working to change U.S. diplomacy. They hoped they could force the Soviet Union into a more cooperative position by opening U.S. relations with China.

Henry Kissinger speaking at Tel Aviv University, Israel, in 1983.

After Nixon was forced to resign by the Watergate scandal, Kissinger served President Gerald Ford as secretary of state. He tried to negotiate a peace settlement in the Middle East. However, he could not find an end to the conflict between Israel and its Arab neighbors. Kissinger left office in 1976, but he continued to work as a writer, lecturer, and adviser on foreign policy and business. Henry Kissinger was the most important figure in American foreign policy in the 1970s. He received the Nobel Peace Prize in 1973 for his peace efforts in Vietnam.

A Peace Plan for Vietnam

Meanwhile, Kissinger continued his talks in France with North Vietnam's Le Duc Tho during 1972. Late in the year—perhaps because an election loomed—Nixon told him to make a key concession. The United States would no longer insist that all North Vietnamese troops must leave the South before all American troops would be withdrawn. On October 26, less than two weeks before the election, Kissinger announced that "peace is at hand."

But the government of South Vietnam would not agree to the terms of the peace, and a few weeks later the deal was off. In December 1972, the United States launched the heaviest

When the Vietnam Veterans' Memorial in Washington, D.C., was dedicated in 1982, the public attitude to Vietnam veterans changed somewhat. Many people were moved by "the Wall," a slab of granite etched with the names of all Americans who had died in the Vietnam War. There was a growing realization among those who had opposed the war that the men who had fought and died in Vietnam were worthy of honor and respect.

bombing of North Vietnam ever. At the same time, it put pressure on the government of South Vietnam to agree to the peace plan. Nixon promised the president of South Vietnam that the United States would respond "with full force" if the North broke the peace. On January 27, 1973, a peace agreement was signed. The Vietnam War was over, at least for the United States.

The Aftermath

The peace did not last. Fighting between North and South resumed almost immediately. Two years later, North Vietnam launched an all-out invasion of South Vietnam. Congress blocked any effort to provide military assistance to the South, which was quickly overrun. In April 1975, the government of South Vietnam surrendered. The victorious North renamed Saigon as Ho Chi Minh City. Vietnam had been unified as a communist state.

The cost of the war to the United States was high. More than 58,000 Americans were killed, and 365,000 were wounded. Some U.S. soldiers had been held in Vietnam for years as prisoners of war. Even those without physical wounds suffered. Many were scarred emotionally by their experiences. Others became bitter when they came home, because antiwar feelings were so strong that many returning veterans were shunned or criticized.

A lasting effect of Vietnam was a loss of respect for and confidence in the national government. Stories about lies and deceptions by government officials during the war made it harder for citizens to accept leaders' statements afterward.

The Lessons of Vietnam

In the 1990s, former Defense Secretary Robert McNamara wrote a memoir in which he said, "We were wrong, terribly wrong." But what, exactly, was the administration wrong about? Politicians, generals, and ordinary Americans argued many times after the war about the "lessons of Vietnam." They do not always agree on what those lessons are.

To some, Vietnam demonstrates that the United States should never become involved in a foreign civil war. Others say that American leaders should have tried to understand and respond to the unique conditions that brought about civil war in Vietnam. Some analysts point to the suffering inflicted on South Vietnam after the North's victory. They say that the United States was right to become involved but should have committed completely to the fight.

Vietnam taught lessons also about the relative power of president and Congress. Members of Congress were upset with President Johnson's conduct of the war, and Nixon's secret bombing of Cambodia had angered them further. Late in 1973, Congress moved to stop presidents from using troops without its approval. Under the War Powers Act passed that year, presidents could respond to emergencies without prior authorization by Congress. They did, however, have to ask Congress for that authority within two days of committing troops. An undeclared war like Vietnam, Congress said, would not be fought again.

The Fall of Richard Nixon

Long unpopular with a large segment of the population, Richard Nixon was elected by only a narrow majority in 1968. As president, he faced antiwar protests and criticism from the press. And he saw government secrets being printed in newspapers while he tried to conduct delicate peace talks. Nixon developed a tendency to see people as friends or as enemies. His desire to strike back at those enemies proved to be his downfall.

Nixon's Domestic Policy

The Great Society of Lyndon Johnson had aroused fears among many conservatives, including Nixon, about the growing power of the federal government. To counter the growth of federal power, Nixon pushed a plan he called "the new federalism." He wanted Washington to give money to state and local governments and allow them to choose how to spend it. This practice was called revenue sharing.

To win support, Nixon took some actions favored by the Democrats, who controlled Congress. Funding for social security, Medicare and Medicaid, and food programs for the poor all increased. Nixon also backed new laws to protect the environment.

Sometimes, when Congress authorized funds for programs Nixon did not support, he simply didn't spend the money. His actions were challenged in the Supreme Court, which ruled they were unconstitutional. Nixon responded by doing away with the Office of Economic Opportunity. Democrats' opposition to his policies increased.

The Birth of the Environmental Movement

The environmental movement was born in 1962. That year, biologist and writer Rachel Carson published *Silent Spring*. In her book, Carson detailed the dangers of DDT, a powerful chemical used to kill insects. It was first used during World War II to protect soldiers and civilians from disease-carrying mosquitos. After the war, farmers used DDT to protect their crops from pests. But widespread use of DDT also caused devastation to bird and fish populations across America. Eventually, the use of DDT was banned in the United States.

Carson's book spurred Americans to look at air and water pollution. Then, in the late 1960s, oil on the heavily polluted Cuyahoga River near Cleveland, Ohio, actually caught fire. Images of the burning river shocked American citizens.

On April 22, 1970, millions of Americans celebrated the first "Earth Day," showing their desire to clean up pollution and protect natural resources. More than 10,000 schools and 2,000 colleges staged events aimed at increasing public awareness of environmental issues. Nixon organized the Environmental Protection Agency (EPA) to oversee federal efforts to clean up the environment. He also signed the Clean Air Act of 1970 and several other laws.

Children cleaning up a city park on the first Earth Day in 1970.

Nixon also angered Democrats on civil rights. He ordered the Justice Department to delay the push for integration in South Carolina and Mississippi. In 1972, the Supreme Court said this went against their rulings and ordered him to stop.

In another decision, the Court approved a plan to bus students to schools outside their neighborhoods to achieve integration. Nixon announced he was opposed to this effort.

Nixon's stands on civil rights were part of a "Southern strategy," an effort to gain the support of Southern whites for the Republican party. (Traditionally, Southern whites voted for the Democrats because the Republican party had been founded to oppose the Southern system of slavery in the nineteenth century.) His aim was to pry these voters away from the Democratic party and guarantee his reelection. Nixon also tried to nominate more conservative justices to the Supreme Court. Two of these nominees, both from the South, were rejected by the Senate.

As part of the busing program of the early 1970s, these students were brought on a school bus from white communities to a school in an African American neighborhood of Berkeley, California. Many people, including President Nixon, were opposed to what they saw as forced integration.

The 1972 Election Campaign

As the nation approached the 1972 election, Nixon was in a strong position. Opposition to the Vietnam War was not as vocal as in 1967 and 1968. Tens of thousands of troops had come home, and peace talks were going on. Nixon had won diplomatic success in China and the Soviet Union. His election campaign raised millions of dollars.

The Democratic nomination was gained by a liberal, Senator George McGovern of South Dakota. He seemed linked to the forces of change that were sweeping American society, or—as it appeared to many Americans—that were tearing American society apart.

Despite his advantages over McGovern, Nixon worried about his reelection. Many Americans still did not trust him. Leaks continued to appear in newspapers, which angered Nixon. He felt that liberals in the government were trying to sabotage his presidency.

Break-In at Watergate

People in the White House felt they were at war against forces that would do anything to defeat them. Members of the presidential staff put together lists of "enemies," those politicians and reporters who opposed the administration. The Special Investigations Unit—nicknamed "the Plumbers"—began taking illegal actions. They planted wiretaps on the phones of journalists, hoping to discover who was leaking information. They broke into the office of the psychiatrist of the man who had leaked the Pentagon Papers to *The New York Times*, hoping to find some damaging information.

The Plumbers then broke into the offices of the Democratic National Committee at the Watergate office complex in Washington, D.C. They looked at documents and placed wiretaps on the telephones that would enable them to listen in on conversations. But the wiretaps didn't work, and the intruders went back for a second attempt. The night they returned, on June 17, 1972, they were caught.

The break-in had been ordered by top aides to Nixon. The leader of the burglars worked for the Committee to Re-Elect the President (CREEP), Nixon's campaign organization. Workers in the White House and CREEP worried that any link between the administration and the burglars would damage the president. They began to cover up the connection.

Meanwhile, Nixon's popularity rose as McGovern was painted as an undependable liberal. Kissinger's October statement that peace was at hand in Vietnam helped the president even more. In November, Nixon won a huge election victory. He won the electoral votes of 49 states and gained almost 61 percent of the popular vote.

Watergate Revealed

On January 20, 1973, Richard Nixon was inaugurated for his second term as president. About the same time, the Watergate burglars were being tried by federal judge John J. Sirica. All pleaded guilty. On February 7, the Senate voted to carry out an investigation of the Watergate affair.

Sirica, a tough judge, knew the burglars were hiding something. One of the burglars, James W. McCord—a former CIA agent—had written a letter to Sirica, admitting that

Bob Woodward (b. 1943) and Carl Bernstein (b. 1944)

Although they were just ordinary news reporters in 1972, Bob Woodward and Carl Bernstein eventually became two of the most famous journalists in the country. Their stories about Watergate in the Washington *Post* newspaper kept the scandal alive for many months.

Woodward had joined the *Post* as a reporter just a few months before the Watergate break-in. Bernstein was a college dropout who had worked on newspapers from the age of 16. Two days after the Watergate break-in, they published their first joint story. It linked the Watergate break-in to Nixon's campaign organization, CREEP. Bernstein found out that $25,000 paid to the burglars came from CREEP. The two reporters published more than 200 stories on Watergate and the cover-up. They won many prizes for journalism, including the Pulitzer Prize. Their books—*All the President's Men* (1974) and *The Final Days* (1976)—became best-sellers.

Bernstein eventually left the *Post* and, after working for a while as an ABC News reporter, left journalism altogether. Woodward remained at the *Post* and became one of its top editors. He has written several other successful books about Washington politics.

"Others involved in the Watergate operation were not identified during the trial. . . . There was political pressure applied to the defendants to plead guilty and remain silent."

James McCord, letter to Judge Sirica, March 1973

he had lied under oath and that others were involved. On March 23, Sirica announced very harsh prison sentences. He said he would cut the sentences if the men cooperated with the Senate investigation.

A month later, Nixon tried to end all speculation about the Watergate case. He announced that he was accepting the resignations of two close aides and that he was firing a White House attorney. All three had played important roles in covering up the connection between the burglars and Nixon's team. Nixon also announced that a special prosecutor would investigate the matter.

Beginning in May 1973, and all during the summer, Senate committee hearings into the Watergate affair were televised. A Republican senator expressed what many Americans wondered: "What did the president know, and when did he know it?" The senators questioned many of the president's aides. Their answers revealed the enemies' lists, the unlawful break-ins, and the taking of illegal campaign contributions. These actions suggested that the Nixon administration, while publicly supporting law and order, actually had contempt for the law.

John Dean, the attorney Nixon had fired, was a key witness. He charged that Nixon had ordered the payment of money to the burglars to keep them quiet. Dean also said the president had moved to block the FBI investigation into the burglary. If the charges were true, the president had obstructed justice. Nixon denied any involvement in the cover-up. At one news conference, he declared, "I am not a crook."

The White House Tapes

In July 1973, the Senate committee learned that the White House had a recording system that taped conversations in Nixon's office. The committee immediately asked to have the tapes from key dates in the cover-up.

Nixon refused to turn them over, citing "executive privilege," the idea that the president's conversations had to be kept private. He also said that handing over the tapes would weaken the nation's security. Eventually, in April 1974, Nixon did release written versions of parts of the tapes. He said they proved his innocence, but some conversations implied that the president had been involved in the cover-up.

On July 24, 1974, the Supreme Court ruled that the president had to hand over the tapes. Meanwhile, the Judiciary Committee of the House of Representatives had been debating whether the charges against the president should lead to his removal from office, or impeachment. On July 27, the committee decided that there were indeed grounds for impeachment.

During the Watergate hearings in 1973, the Senate committee, led by Senator Sam Ervin, listens to the testimony of John Ehrlichman, formerly the president's adviser on domestic affairs. Ehrlichman was suspected of being involved in the cover-up of the Watergate break-ins. He was later convicted of conspiracy, perjury (lying under oath), and obstruction of justice.

On August 5, the president released the tapes, as the Court had ordered. Transcripts showed that just a few days after the break-in, Nixon had authorized the payment of money to the burglars to buy their silence. He had also moved to block the FBI investigation.

At this point, Republicans in Congress abandoned Nixon. It was clear that he would be impeached and removed from office. But on August 9, 1974, Richard Nixon became the first president in United States history to resign his office.

Richard Nixon makes a farewell speech on August 9, 1974, having announced that he was resigning the office of president the day before. His wife Pat (left), his daughter Tricia, and his son-in-law Edward Cox stand behind him at the podium.

The Unelected President

During the Watergate investigation, Vice President Spiro Agnew had had his own troubles. In 1973, he was investigated on charges of corruption stemming from his days as governor of Maryland. In October 1973, he pleaded "no contest" to the charges. Though not a guilty plea, it meant that Agnew was not fighting the charges. Discredited, he resigned from office, the first vice president ever to do so.

To take Agnew's place, Nixon appointed Representative Gerald R. Ford of Michigan. The Senate quickly approved Ford, who became the nation's first unelected vice president. When Nixon resigned, Ford took the presidential oath of office. He was the first person ever to lead the nation without having been elected as vice president or president.

Ford worried that Watergate would continue to grab the nation's attention if Nixon faced criminal charges. He felt that he and Congress had to address many problems that had been overlooked for too long. In early September 1974, Ford gave Nixon a full pardon for any and all crimes that he had committed as president. The action was highly controversial, but Ford weathered the protests.

"Our long national nightmare is over."

Gerald Ford,
August 8, 1974

Ford Faces Problems

Ford faced a long list of problems. In the early 1970s, the oil-producing nations of the Middle East had raised the price of crude oil, which is used to make gasoline, heating oil, and other products. These steep price hikes had jarred the American economy.

Inflation was running high, and unemployment was rising as well. A new word, "stagflation," was used to describe the combination of high inflation and a stagnant, or non-growing, economy. The problem was especially bad in the industrialized areas of the Northeast and Midwest, which were being hit by

Betty Ford (b. 1918)

Betty Ford trained as a dancer in her youth. She married Gerald Ford in 1948. He was elected to the House of Representatives shortly after their marriage, and the Fords spent most of the next 30 years in Washington.

When Ford became president, his wife offered a refreshing dose of honesty and plain speaking. Though in many ways a conservative, Betty Ford took aggressive positions. She supported a woman's right to abortion. She also backed the Equal Rights Amendment, a controversial proposal to add an amendment to the Constitution that would secure equal rights for women.

One of Ford's most important actions was to be honest about having breast cancer, a disease that was only beginning to be widely talked about. Her openness helped spur many women to seek tests and treatment for themselves. Many women said Ford's example saved their lives.

After Gerald Ford was no longer president, Betty Ford again showed courage on a difficult topic. She admitted to having become addicted to alcohol and pain killers. With her successful rehabilitation, Ford once again set an important example for other Americans. She also helped found an effective facility for treating people with addictions.

Betty Ford at the Republican convention in 1976.

growing competition from foreign products. As factories closed, this region came to be called "the Rust Belt." People were abandoning these areas for southern and western regions. And while the anger of the Vietnam years had abated, there were still deep divisions and turmoil in American society.

President Ford next to the Bicentennial Bell in New York Harbor in 1976.

War and Peace in the Middle East

One of Ford's biggest problems was the continuing conflict in the Middle East. Problems there reflected, and were affected by, the Cold War. After World War II, the victorious Allies, horrified by the wartime persecution of Jews, agreed to allow Jews to settle in their ancient homeland in British-controlled Palestine. In 1948, the state of Israel was created. The United States was the first country to recognize the new Jewish nation.

Arabs living in the area were angered by these events. Creating a Jewish homeland meant displacing the Palestinian Arabs who lived there or placing them under Israeli rule. Several of Israel's neighbors attacked but, with American aid, the new nation managed to survive.

War struck the region again in 1956 and once more in 1967. That year, Israel was victorious, defeating its far more numerous Arab neighbors. Israel also seized some territory from the Arab nations of Egypt, Jordan, and Syria, and refused to give it back. As a result, perhaps a million more Palestinians were under Israeli rule, and many thousands fled to become refugees in neighboring countries.

The United States was one of Israel's most firm backers. For many years, the Arab nations received support from the Soviet Union. In the 1970s, though, Richard Nixon and Henry Kissinger established closer relations with the Arab states. Kissinger tried "shuttle diplomacy," flying from one capital to another in the region. These moves were not enough, however, to forge a lasting peace in the Middle East.

Conclusion

The United States had weathered several crises since the end of World War II. It had participated in wars abroad, faced growing unrest at home, and experienced great changes in society. In the early 1970s, Americans were faced with economic problems at home and challenges in their relationship with the rest of the world.

Americans rallied briefly in 1976 to celebrate the nation's bicentennial, or the 200th anniversary of its independence. Local and national groups across the country commemorated the history of the people who had settled there and founded a new nation. Parades, fireworks, concerts, and other events allowed people to show their pride in being Americans and their relief at surviving all their recent problems and turmoil.

But deep questions lingered. Hispanics, African Americans, Native Americans, and women pointed out that the nation was still plagued by inequality. Confidence had been shaken by the violence of the 1960s, the divisions caused by the Vietnam War, and the constitutional crisis raised by Watergate. The economy stumbled along, and people feared the return of the Great Depression.

Americans were worried that the nation was in decline. In the full flush of victory in World War II, a journalist had declared the opening of "the American century." In 1976, barely 30 years later, Americans wondered if that period was already ending.

Fireworks light up the night sky over Washington, D.C., during the 1976 bicentennial celebrations.

Glossary

boycott	To refuse to deal with a person or group, or to buy certain products, as a form of protest.
budget	The amount of money available for a particular purpose.
capitalism	An economic system in which property and resources are privately owned and in which people operate businesses for profit.
communism	A political system in which people should share common ownership of all resources and property and everyone should work for the good of the whole community.
conservative	A person whose political approach is traditional and opposed to extreme reforms.
consumer	A buyer or user of goods or services.
democratic	Describes a system in which people are their own authority rather than being ruled over by an unelected leader. In a democratic system, people vote on decisions and rules, or elect representatives to vote for them.
depression	A time when the economy of a country or region goes into a severe decline, resulting in very low production and high unemployment.
desegregation	The elimination or official banning of segregation.
dictator	A ruler who has absolute power and authority.
discrimination	The favoring of one group above another.
economic	To do with the economy, meaning the production and use of goods and services, and the system of money that is used for the flow of goods and services.
environmental	To do with the surrounding world, and often used to describe issues concerning the natural world and its protection.
federal	To do with the central, or national, government of a country rather than the regional, or state, governments.
feminist	A person who believes in equal rights for women.
immigrant	A person who has left the country of his or her birth and come to live in another country.
impeachment	The process by which Congress can remove public officials from office.
inflation	A rise in prices due usually to an increase in the amount of money in circulation when there is no similar increase in the amount of available goods and services.

integration	The bringing of a person or group of people into another, larger group as equals.
intervene	To interfere or get involved in the political affairs of another nation.
labor union	An organization of workers that exists to improve the working conditions of its members and negotiate on their behalf with employers.
legislation	Laws, or the making of laws.
liberal	A political attitude that supports progress and reform in society and the involvement of government in the welfare and civil rights of citizens.
minimum wage	The hourly wage that is the lowest possible that any business can pay to a worker according to national law.
nationalist	A person with strong loyalty to his or her country, its culture, and its independence.
offensive	A military attack.
policy	A plan or way of doing things that is decided on, and then used in managing situations, making decisions, or tackling problems.
primary	An election to nominate a candidate for political office or select delegates to attend a political convention.
radical	A person who favors distinct political, economic, or social changes or reform.
reform	A change intended to improve conditions.
segregation	The policy of keeping people from different racial or ethnic groups separate, usually with one group having fewer rights than another.
sociologists	Scientists who study how society affects people's lives and behavior.
technology	The knowledge and ability that improves ways of doing practical things. A person performing a task using any tool, from a wooden spoon to the most complicated computer, is applying technology.
unconstitutional	An action or law not authorized by the Constitution.
veteran	A person who served for a long time at a job, particularly in the military, or who served on a specific campaign or expedition.
veto	To use authority by refusing to approve or allow something. For instance, a president can refuse to approve laws that have been passed in Congress.

Time Line

1945	United Nations formed.
	World War II ends.
	President Harry Truman presents Fair Deal policies.
1946	Supreme Court rules in favor of integration.
1947	Truman begins policy of containment, and Marshall Plan begins.
	Taft-Hartley Act passed.
1948	Berlin Airlift.
	Truman reelected president.
1949	NATO formed, creating alliance of Western nations.
1950	Korean War begins.
1952	Dwight Eisenhower elected president.
1953	CIA helps overthrow government in Iran.
	Cease-fire in Korea.
1954	*Brown v. Board of Education of Topeka* rules against school segregation.
	CIA helps overthrow government in Guatemala.
	Arms race begins.
1955	Warsaw Pact creates alliance of communist nations.
	Montgomery bus boycott begins.
1957	Eisenhower sends federal troops to integrate high school in Little Rock, Arkansas.
1960	First sit-in in Greensboro, North Carolina, leads to other sit-ins.
	Soviets shoot down U.S. spy plane.
	John F. Kennedy elected president.
1961	Bay of Pigs invasion.
	First manned U.S. space flights.
1962	John Glenn makes first American manned orbit of Earth.
	Cuban Missile Crisis.
1963	U.S. and Soviet Union agree to ban some nuclear testing.
	Civil rights march to Washington, D.C.
	Kennedy assassinated, and Lyndon Johnson becomes president.
	National Farm Workers Association founded by Cesar Chavez.
	Equal Pay Act passed.
1964	Civil Rights Act passed.
	Race riots in Harlem, New York City.

1964   Americans and North Vietnamese boats clash in Gulf of Tonkin.
        Gulf of Tonkin Resolution.
        Johnson elected president.
1965   Johnson sends more troops to Vietnam and begins bombing campaign.
        Antiwar movement begins.
        Congress passes Great Society bills, including Medicare and Medicaid.
        Voting Rights Act passed.
        Race riots in Los Angeles.
1967   "Summer of Love" in San Francisco.
1968   U.S. taxes increased to pay for war in Vietnam.
        Tet Offensive.
        My Lai Massacre.
        Martin Luther King, Jr., and Robert Kennedy assassinated.
        Richard Nixon elected president.
        Indian Civil Rights Act passed.
1969   Nixon begins withdrawal of troops from Vietnam.
        Neil Armstrong and Buzz Aldrin achieve first moon landing.
1970   U.S. invades Cambodia.
        Renewed antiwar protests lead to shootings at colleges in Ohio and
        Mississippi.
        Environmental Protection Agency (EPA) founded.
        Clean Air Act passed.
        Gulf of Tonkin Resolution repealed.
1971   Pentagon Papers published by newspapers.
1972   Nixon visits China and Soviet Union.
        Watergate break-in.
        Nixon reelected president.
        Equal Employment Opportunity Act passed.
1973   Paris peace agreement ends U.S. participation in Vietnam War.
        Investigations into Watergate cover-up begin.
        Vice President Spiro Agnew resigns.
        War Powers Act passed.
1974   Nixon resigns, and Gerald R. Ford becomes president.
1976   United States celebrates bicentennial.

Further Reading

Blau, Justine. *Betty Friedan: Feminist* (Women of Achievement Series). Broomall, PA: Chelsea House, 1990.

Cohen, Daniel. *Watergate: Deception in the White House* (Spotlight on American History Series). Brookfield, CT: Millbrook Press, 1998.

Dolan, Edward F. *America in the Korean War*. Brookfield, CT: Millbrook Press, 1998.

Dudley, William. *The Vietnam War: Opposing Viewpoints* (Opposing Viewpoints Series). San Diego, CA: Greenhaven Press, 1997.

Stein, Conrad R. *The Great Red Scare* (American Events Series). Parsippany, NJ: Silver Burdett Press, 1997.

Super, Neil. *Vietnam War Soldiers* (African American Soldiers Series). New York: 21st Century Books, 1995.

Warren, James A. *Cold War: The American Crusade Against the Soviet Union and World Communism, 1945–1990*. New York: Lothrop, Lee and Shephard, 1996.

Weber, Michael. *Causes and Consequences of the African American Civil Rights Movement* (Causes and Consequences Series). Austin, TX: Raintree Steck-Vaughn, 1998.

Websites

Watergate 25 – Timeline, photos, contemporary accounts, and biographies of the major figures in the only political scandal to unseat an American president.
http:/www.washingtonpost.com/wp-srv/national/longterm/watergate

The American Experience: Vietnam Online – Online history of the VietnamWar, told through film, photographs, interviews, and historical analysis. Includes the Vietnamese perspective.
http://www.pbs.org/wgbh/pages/amex/vietnam

The Cuban Missile Crisis – Timeline, photos, analysis, and archival documents relating to the confrontation that nearly plunged the world into nuclear war.
http://www.hyperion.advanced.org

Bibliography

Boller, Paul, Jr. *Presidential Campaigns*, rev. ed. New York: Oxford University Press, 1996.

Brinkley, Douglas. *American History: A Survey*. New York: McGraw-Hill, 1993.

Danzer, Gerald A., and others. *The Americans*. Evanston, IL.: McDougal Littell, 1998.

Goldman, Eric F. *The Tragedy of Lyndon Johnson*. New York: Dell, 1974.

Halberstam, David. *The Fifties*. New York: Fawcett Columbine, 1993.

Karnow, Stanley. *Vietnam: A History*. Boston, MA: Little, Brown, 1983.

Katz, William Loren. *Eyewitness*, rev. and updated. New York: Simon & Schuster, 1995.

Kendrick, Alexander. *The Wound Within: America in the Vietnam Years, 1945–1974*. Boston, MA: Little, Brown, 1974.

Manchester, William. *The Glory and the Dream: A Narrative History of America, 1932–1972*. Boston, MA: Little, Brown, 1974.

O'Brien, Steven G. *American Political Leaders: From Colonial Times to the Present*. Santa Barbara, CA: ABC-CLIO, 1991.

Schlesinger, Arthur M., Jr., ed. *The Almanac of American History*, rev. and updated. New York: Barnes and Noble Books, 1993.

White, Theodore H. *Breach of Faith: The Fall of Richard Nixon*. New York: Dell, 1975.

Index